DISCOVERING COTSWOLD VILLAGES

Gordon Ottewell

Copyright © 1997, G. Ottewell

Reprinted (with revisions) 2001

All Rights Reserved. No part of this publication may be reproduced, stored in a retrieval system, or transmitted in any form or by any means – electronic, mechanical, photocopying, recording, or otherwise – without prior written permission from the publisher.

First published by Sigma Leisure (1997)

British Library Cataloguing in Publication Data
A CIP record for this book is available from the British Library.

ISBN: 978-0-9510586-6-4

This edition published by Barn Owl Books 2007

Typesetting and Design by: Sigma Press, Wilmslow, Cheshire.

Cover Design: MFP Design & Print

Cover Photograph: Arlington Row, Bibury (Gordon Ottewell)

Illustrations: Alec Betterton

Printed and bound in Great Britain by
Antony Rowe Ltd, Chippenham, Wiltshire.

Preface

> "All things in Cotswold possess a unity whose primary source is the quality and nature of its limestone."
>
> *H.J. Massingham, 'Wold Without End' 1932.*

The Cotswolds lay claim to a higher proportion of well-known villages than any other English region. Their names – Broadway, Bourton-on-the-Water, Bibury, Stanway, Stanton, the Slaughters, the Swells – have been familiar to generations of tourists and their limestone buildings will no doubt continue to grace countless calendars, postcards and coffee-table picture books for generations to come.

Ask visitors why they find the Cotswolds so alluring and more often than not they will cite the beauty of the region's stone built churches, manor houses and cottages. True, many will also enthuse about the charming towns, the scenery, the lovely river valleys, woodland and wildlife, but it is without doubt the glory of the villages, their stone blooming in the sun, that accounts for a great deal of the Cotswolds' appeal.

Although much has been written about these villages, there is as yet no practical guidebook to assist the visitor to discover their delights on foot. The aim of this book is to fill that gap. I have selected 50 villages, scattered across the Cotswolds, that are ideally suited to on-foot exploration. Some are well known, others less so. Some popular villages, such as Broadway and Bourton-on-the-Water, are omitted, simply to make room for other, equally appealing, though less well known alternatives.

The included villages are arranged in groups according to their proximity to the nearest town. A sketchmap of each group appears at the start of the section with notes on the relevant town. Following location details and a brief introductory description, highlights of the history of the village are included. Finally comes a carefully planned and described walkabout, designed to enable the reader to gain the maximum enjoyment from the visit.

Indeed, the word enjoyment summarises the primary aim of the book. Cotswold villages need to be explored slowly, patiently, with time to stand and stare. Do this and you cannot fail to find deep and lasting enjoyment in your exploration.

Gordon Ottewell, Winchcombe

Contents

Notes on the Discovery Trails	**1**
Chipping Campden Area	**3**
Blockley	*5*
Broad Campden	*8*
Ilmington	*11*
Snowshill	*14*
Weston-sub-Edge	*17*
Willersey	*20*
Winchcombe Area	**23**
Guiting Power	*25*
Hawling	*28*
Sevenhampton and Brockhampton	*31*
Stanton	*34*
Stanway	*37*
Stow-on-the-Wold Area	**40**
Adlestrop	*42*
Bledington	*45*
Broadwell	*48*
Chastleton	*51*
Churchill	*54*
Condicote	*57*
Great Rissington	*60*
Icomb	*63*
Kingham	*66*
Little Rissington	*69*
Naunton	*72*
Oddington	*75*

The Slaughters	*78*
Wyck Rissington	*82*

Northleach Area — 85
Chedworth	*87*
Compton Abdale	*90*
Notgrove	*93*
Sherborne	*96*
Withington	*99*

Burford Area — 102
Asthall	*104*
Filkins and Broughton Poggs	*107*
Great Barrington	*110*
Little Barrington	*113*
Minster Lovell (Old Minster)	*116*
Shilton	*119*
Shipton-under-Wychwood	*122*
Swinbrook and Widford	*125*
Westwell	*128*
Windrush	*131*

Fairford Area — 134
Bibury	*136*
Coln St Aldwyns	*139*
The Eastleaches	*142*
Southrop	*145*

Stroud and Tetbury Area — 148
Avening	*150*
Beverston	*153*
Bisley	*156*
Chalford	*159*
Sapperton	*162*
Uley and Owlpen	*165*

Appendix — 168

Notes on the Discovery Trails

The actual village trails, referred to in the text as walkabouts, vary both in length and form, depending on the interest-potential and layout of the villages themselves. Wherever possible, the retracing of steps is avoided but as a satisfactory circular route is impossible in certain of the villages, some repetition is inevitable.

As to the amount of time required, most walkabouts can be completed well within an hour. However, in the author's opinion there is so much to see in the selected villages that many visitors will require considerably longer, not necessarily to walk, but just to savour the atmosphere.

Some of the walkabouts involve short stretches of field path walking, which can be muddy after rain. A note to this effect is included, wherever appropriate, at the start of the walk directions.

In almost every case, a visit to the village church is recommended. Sadly, the increase in theft and vandalism has led to many churches being kept locked, sometimes with no instructions as to how to obtain keys. In the author's experience, however, polite enquiries soon locate keyholders, who are without exception both helpful and informative.

Church guides, like the churches themselves, vary enormously. All are well worth their modest cost and some provide additional information on the history of the village, supplementing the limited detail contained through lack of space in this book.

Some villages boast their own guide. Again, a wide range of publications are on offer and should be enquired about in village shops, post offices and pubs. The latter, incidentally, often provide not only welcome sustenance on discovery trails but may also display on their walls illuminating insights into the past through old photographs, maps and even artefacts.

Using the area sketchmaps

The simplified area sketchmaps, drawn to a scale of 1: 100000, are included merely to provide a basic general outline of the Cotswolds region and to show the particular location of the selected villages. These featured villages are shown in heavy type, whereas other villages within the area are shown in lighter type.

Some overlap of the areas, based as they are on prominent towns, is unavoidable. It should also be pointed out that as the included villages were chosen for their suitability for on-foot exploration, their distribution is such that the sketchmaps do not provide coverage of the entire

Cotswold region. It will be noted, for instance, that neither Cirencester nor Painswick is included, simply because villages in their vicinity have for convenience been grouped with others centred on nearby towns.

Any detailed exploration of the British countryside is greatly enhanced by reference to Ordnance Survey maps. Accordingly, the relevant Landranger sheet number, followed by a six-figure grid reference, is given for the suggested parking and starting point in each village included.

Chipping Campden Area

Bordering on the Vale of Evesham and the Stour valley of Warwickshire, this is the most northerly area of the Cotswolds. The scenery is extremely varied, ranging from the low-lying north western fringes to a stretch of upland wold at the summit of Fish Hill, Broadway, rising to over 320 metres above sea level at Broadway Tower Country Park.

The villages of the area reflect the varied scenery. The rich golden stone of the upland villages gives way on the lower slopes to houses and cottages of mellow brick, with thatch a distinguishing feature.

Broadway, the largest village in the area, has been a tourist haven since Victorian times. There is no denying the beauty of its main street, with elegant houses of the local limestone climbing towards the escarpment. It has long since forfeited any claim to be a typical Cotswold village however, and has therefore been omitted from the selected list.

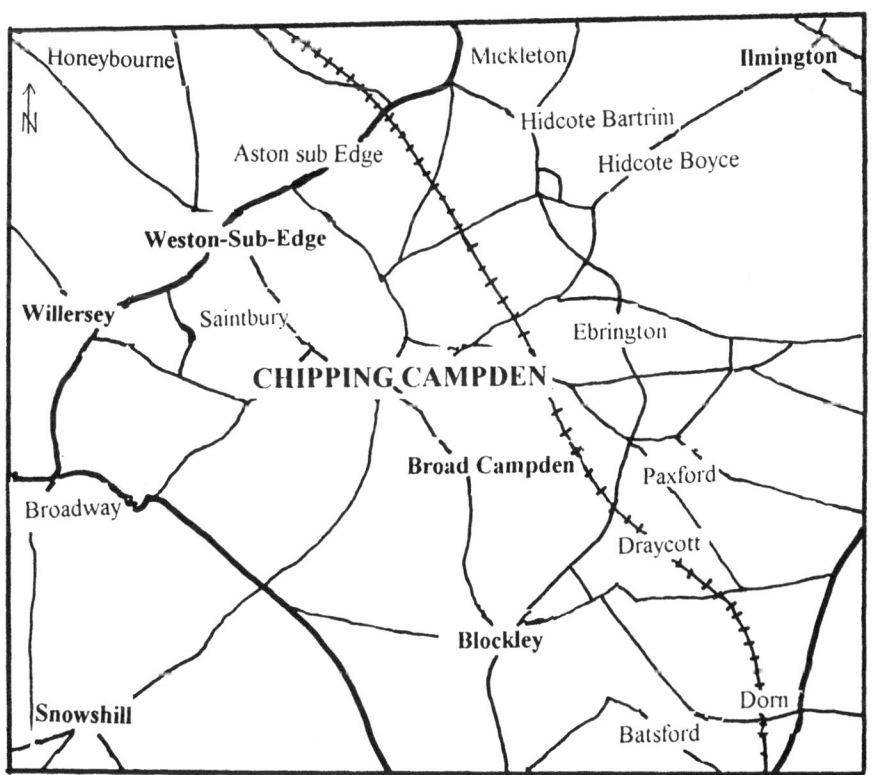

National Trust properties in the area include Snowshill Manor, a fine Tudor house set in attractive gardens containing an amazing assortment of bygones collected by the eccentric Charles Wade; Dover's Hill, scene of the 'Cotswold Olympick Games' founded in the 17th century by Robert Dover; and Hidcote Manor Gardens, a series of formal gardens enclosed by hedges, with rare trees and shrubs.

Close to Hidcote are Kiftsgate Court Gardens, privately owned and commanding fine views with unusual trees and shrubs and featuring the celebrated Kiftsgate rose.

Chipping Campden

This small market town is generally acknowledged as being one of the finest architectural treasures of the Cotswolds. It was built largely by wealthy medieval wool merchants and among its exceptionally fine buildings are the Perpendicular 'wool' church, 17th century almshouses, the lodges and gatehouse of Sir Baptist Hicks's great mansion destroyed during the Civil War, the Woolstaplers' Hall, William Grevel's house (14th century) and the much photographed Market Hall dating from 1627.

The town was the birthplace of Edward ('Chinese') Wilson, the distinguished plant collector, and a memorial garden in his name can be visited at the north end of the High Street.

Chipping Campden marks the northern extremity of the Cotswold Way long-distance footpath, which stretches for 105 miles from Bath. It is also on the Heart of England Way, which extends for almost 100 miles from Cannock Chase in Staffordshire through the north Cotswolds to Bourton-on-the-Water.

Blockley

Getting there:	Blockley lies on the B4479, 3 miles SE of Chipping Campden and 3 miles NW of Moreton-in-Marsh.
Park:	In or near Post Office Square, near the church. (O.S. Landranger Sheet 151. GR 164350)
Introducing the Village:	Totally unlike any other north Cotswold village, Blockley was once a silk-manufacturing centre, with mills lining the valley of the Blockley Brook and with terraces of workers' cottages clinging to the hillside above. The surviving mill buildings have long since been converted into spacious residences and the cottages have become the homes of outsiders seeking country life. Fortunately, both mills and cottages were well built of the local apricot-coloured stone, with the result that this large village combines scenic attractiveness with an exceptionally interesting history.
Refreshments:	Great Western Inn. Crown Inn. Old Coach House Tearoom.

A peep into the past

The manor of Blockley was bought by the Bishop of Worcester in the 9th century and remained part of Worcestershire until its transfer to Gloucestershire in 1931. Successive bishops kept up to 2,000 sheep in Blockley's pastures, selling the wool to wealthy staplers in Chipping Campden.

Corn mills were recorded on the Blockley Brook in Domesday Book. By the late 17th century, however, silk throwing had been introduced by James Rushout, the son of a Flemish immigrant. This trade prospered, as did the Rushouts, the fourth son in the line becoming the first Lord Northwick, and by 1824, 8 silk mills, employing some 800 hands, were engaged in production for the Coventry ribbon trade.

Eventually the silk trade boom was killed by foreign competition and by 1885, the mills were converted to other uses – corn milling, wood-sawing and even piano manufacture. These industries, too, withered and Blockley, despite being one of the first villages in the country to produce its own electricity, generated from the powerful flow of the Blockley Brook, settled into a period of decline from which it has only recently emerged as a sought-after retirement haven and congenial commuter village.

Walkabout

1. Several interesting features can be seen from Post Office Square. Above on the left is the bowling green, said to be the only level ground

Blockley church from the Square

Chipping Campden Area

in the village. Below stands an unusual modern dovecote, built on to a garage. This won a Civic Award in 1959. Mill Close pond was created to serve a silk mill and was later employed to generate electricity. The building to the right of the church approach, now a tearoom and nursery school, was built as a stable and coach house in 1709 and later became a charity school.

2. Enter the churchyard. Many of the graves of local dignitaries are enclosed by wrought iron railings. To the south of the churchyard is the rambling 17th century manor house, said to occupy the site of the Bishop of Worcester's summer residence.

3. The church of St Peter and St Paul is a vast structure of dark stone, representing many periods. It retains its Norman chancel but its tower dates only from 1725, and was based on that of Chipping Campden. As well as an extensive range of monuments, chiefly to the Rushouts of Northwick Park, there are two brasses to priests, one of 1405 in the chancel floor, the other, of 1510, on the sedilia.

4. Leave the churchyard at the top left hand corner to reach the Square. Turn left along the High Street, with its raised pavement and handsome terraces of 17th – 19th century houses and cottages.

5. Opposite the historic Crown Inn, with its arched carriageway, stands Tudor House, bearing a Sun Insurance firemark. Further on, beyond the impressive former Ebenezer chapel of 1835, is a fine old house with mullions and dormer windows and bearing the date of 1732 over its ornate doorway.

6. Beyond Russell Spring, from which issued "Water from the living rocks. God's precious gift to man", stands Rock Cottage, its gatepost embellished by a plaque indicating that the prophetess Joanna Southcott lived there for ten years until her death in 1814. Fish Cottage, so named because its garden contains a memorial board to a pet trout, which lived in the garden pond for 20 years, is the last house on the right before High Street gives way to a bridleway through the lovely Dovedale woods.

7. Retrace steps as far as a path on the right, just beyond 'Woolstaplers' and Vale Cottage. This ancient way, known as Donkey Lane, can be followed along the stream and back to rejoin High Street.

8. Turn right and continue as far as Chapel Lane on the left. The climb up this lane is rewarded by good views over the village and valley. Turn right at Back Ends (site of the old fairground) and descend Bell Bank to rejoin High Street opposite the church.

Broad Campden

Getting there:	Broad Campden lies between the B4081 and the B4479, 1 mile SE of Chipping Campden.
Park:	As near as possible to the Baker's Arms Inn (Use car park if patronising inn). (O.S. Landranger Sheet 151. GR 157378).
Introducing the village	Guidebooks vie with one another in lavishing praise on this tiny village of thatched cottages grouped around its own miniature valley. Such words as picturesque, delightful, enchanting – delicious even – have been employed in an attempt to convey Broad Campden's charms. And well they might, for its smallness of scale and snugness of atmosphere render it totally unlike the neighbouring and much visited former wool town, part of whose name it shares and with whose history it is inextricably linked.
Refreshments:	Baker's Arms.

A peep into the past

Although Broad Campden was originally the eastern half of the manor of Chipping Campden, it had its own church by 1150. This church, now Chapel House, was derelict until C.R. Ashbee, a disciple of William Morris and founder of the Chipping Campden Guild of Handicrafts, restored and converted it as the base for his Essex House Press in 1905.

Broad Campden's most illustrious son is undoubtedly Jonathan Hulls, the son of a weaver and small farmer, who was born in 1699. At school he revealed a passionate interest in science and mathematics and as a young man his studies of Newcomen's engine, used for driving water pumps in mines, convinced him that this type of engine could be adapted to propel boats.

Accordingly, in 1736, with the backing of Squire Freeman of Batsford Park, he patented a stream-propelled boat, which was tested on the River Avon at Evesham but which proved unsuccessful. Sadly, Hulls was unable to obtain sufficient funding to continue his experiment and thereafter confined his inventive skills to less spectacular creations, including a slide rule, which enjoyed widespread use for many years.

Jonathan Hulls was a Quaker and on his death in 1758 he was buried in the tiny burial ground of the Friends' meeting house in the village, which had been established almost a century earlier and which is passed on the walkabout.

Chipping Campden Area

The Norman chapel at Broad Campden

Walkabout

This entails a short (quarter of a mile) stretch of field-path walking, which can be muddy after rain.

1. From the Baker's Arms, walk towards the centre of the village. On the right, a gate in the thick yew hedge allows the briefest of glimpses of Chapel House, described as having been 'long a prey to ivy and choked by nettle and brambles' when C.R. Ashbee discovered it and converted it into his home in 1905.

2. Two options are possible from the humpy little village green. The more direct route lies along the public footpath signposted between the two roads to the right of the church. This dips, crosses a stream over a footbridge, and climbs back to the road, which is then followed to the left for a short distance to reach a road signed 'Unsuitable for Motors' on the left.
Alternatively, follow the road as it dips and bends to the right, passing the handsome Malt House, with its latticed windows, dormers and fine finial on the left. As the road swings and climbs, a good view can

now be had of Chapel House, behind its topiaried yew hedge. Continue as far as the unsuitable-for-motors road on the left. The pleasant row of cottages and a farm ahead mark the eastern extremity of the village.

3. Follow the delightful motor-free lane on its switchback meandering course back to the green. It is flanked by ivy and lichen-clad stone walls and shaded by veteran hollies.

4. St Michael's church, angular and severe, dates from 1868. The oak communion rail was designed by C.R. Ashbee.

5. Alongside is Hull's house, former home of Jonathan Hulls. It was substantially enlarged after the inventor's death in 1758.

6. Follow the 'Public footpath to Chipping Campden' sign past the charming row of cottages named after flowers and shrubs on the left. The Quaker meeting house of 1663 is on the right. (Retrace to start to avoid field path walking).

7. The path swings to the left between walls and enters a private garden via a kissing gate. Continue between staddle stones to pass through a second kissing gate.

8. Follow the Heart of England Way sign along the field edge. Bear half left at an old stone stile and continue as far as a road.

9. Turn left back into Broad Campden. The Baker's Arms is on the left.

Ilmington

Getting there: Ilmington lies midway between the A429 and the B4632, 5 miles NE of Chipping Campden.

Park: By the edge of the top green, close to the war memorial. (O.S. Landranger Sheet 151. GR 210433).

Introducing the village
Warwickshire's share of the Cotswolds is modest but there is no denying the quality of Ilmington, the county's one representative in this book. It is a fairly large village, sheltered beneath Windmill Hill and Ilmington Downs, high, open country.
The village itself can be said to be half Cotswold, half vale, for its buildings are a mix of ginger coloured stone and mellow brick, with thatched roofs scattered among those of tile and stone slates. Though not on a main road, it stands at the hub of a tangle of minor ways, some climbing the Cotswold scarp towards Ebrington and Mickleton, while others wriggle their way eastwards in the direction of the Fosse Way and the Stour Valley.

Refreshments: Howard Arms. Red Lion.

A peep into the past

Ilmington has a rich history. Its chalybeate spring could well have brought it fame as a spa but the close proximity of Leamington and Cheltenham ensured that the exploitation of its healing waters was never really successful.

Before the coming of the railways, the village benefited from the building of a horse-drawn tramway linking Moreton-in-Marsh with Stratford-upon-Avon, with a branch to Shipston-on-Stour. The two tracks, which are still traceable, met just outside Ilmington. Although chiefly employed in transporting coal, the tramway also carried passengers, one of whom later wrote: "At what pace we went or whether that pace would be most appropriately calculated in miles to the hour or hours to the mile, we hardly know...we are of the opinion that it would generally have been quite safe to get down and walk a little."

Ilmington was for many years regarded as the Cotswold home of Morris dancing, and in Sam Bennett, 'The Last of the Troubadours', possessed the most accomplished fiddler for miles around. A linked handkerchief dance, 'The Maid of the Mill', is said to have had its origins in the village.

Ilmington – the Street fron the top green

Walkabout

This entails a short stretch (about a quarter of a mile) of avoidable field path walking, which can be muddy after rain.

1. From the war memorial, and facing the church, turn right and walk down to the village street, passing the Roman Catholic church. Cross by the village hall to reach the site of the pound. The plaque on the wall records the date of the enclosure of the village open fields as 1781.

2. Walk along the pavement, passing the fine Elizabethan manor house, to reach the meeting of ways by the Howard Arms, named after the long-established family at nearby Foxcote.

3. Turn sharp left along the no-through-road, which skirts the Manor gardens before joining the path to the church opposite Bevingtons, a charming thatched cottage.

4. Turn right here. The former manorial fishpond on the right provides rich habitat for mallard, coot and moorhen, with yellow iris dominant among a range of aquatic plants.

5. St Mary's Church, standing in a churchyard rich in interesting monuments and shaded by ancient yews, dates from the 11th century. Both the lower section of the tower and the beautiful arches at the west end are of that period, while over the porch can be seen the coat of arms of Simon de Montfort, once patron of the church. Memorials to eminent local families, the Brents and the Palmers, embellish the interior, which is further enhanced by the oak furnishings, the work of Thompson of Yorkshire, whose mouse 'signature' appears in no less than eleven places.

6. Continue through the churchyard to reach a road. The beautiful Dower House is a short distance to the right. The route continues to the left, as far as the hurdle-maker's workshop. (Those wishing to avoid the field path section should turn left here back to the start).

7. Turn to the right of the workshop. Pass Hill Farm and continue up the old road, known locally as Dark Lane, a sunken way shaded by ancient hollies and sycamores. Go through a gate and turn left across a field to a stile.

8. Descend via steps to a road. Cross and go over a stone stile a few metres to the right. At a crossways of paths, turn right. Keep a garden fence on the left, climb a stile, and continue to cross stiles at a plank bridge. Keep a hedge on the left and cross more stiles to reach Tinker's Lane.

9. Turn left. The lane eventually becomes a road, leading past the handsome Crab Mill (dated 1711) back to the start.

Snowshill

Getting there:	Snowshill lies 2½ miles south of Broadway.
Park:	Snowshill Manor car park (National Trust) at northern edge of village. (O.S. Landranger Sheet 150. GR 096340).
Introducing the village	"It sleeps in a hollow of the wolds' breast, wrapped in its grey cloak", was how H.J. Massingham described Snowshill as he descended to it from the Chipping Campden road in the early 1930s. Yet despite snuggling in its hollow, the village is one of the highest in the Cotswolds and in severe winters fully lives up to its name. The towering summit of Oat Hill affords some shelter from the south but its four approach roads are fully exposed to the elements, leaving the village cut off after heavy snowfall. Snowshill is grouped attractively around the humpy churchyard at the meeting of the ways. Close by, in delightful grounds and with superb views, stands the Manor House, given to the National Trust by its eccentric owner Charles Paget Wade, and filled with the spoils of a lifetime of collecting, including tools, armour, toys and musical instruments. This is the obvious attraction but as will be seen on the walkabout, is by no means all that Snowshill has to offer.
Refreshments:	The Snowshill Arms.

A peep into the past

Snowshill is a place well known to archaeologists. It was from a Bronze Age round barrow tomb half a mile south west of the village that a famous collection of weapons, now in the British Museum, was excavated. These include a bronze dagger, a stone battle axe, a spearhead and a rare type of pin.

The village, which of course came into being much later, belonged to Winchcombe Abbey and records show that up to a thousand sheep were grazed in the vicinity in medieval times. By the 16th century, the manor house was already in existence, although its present front was not added until the 18th century. By this time, many of the small, low cottages we see today had appeared, built from locally quarried stone, and a church stood on the green on the site now occupied by the rather gaunt Victorian structure of 1864.

19th century Snowshill was a bustling place. The annual wake, featuring a dinner for all the villagers, was held on the Saturday of Whit week and was followed in June by the St Barnabas celebrations, which included a procession to the church for a special saints-day service. Afterwards came dancing, the highlight of which was the village's own dance, the Snowsle Swedish, still performed into the 1920s by men well into their seventies.

Another ancient tradition that survived longer at remote Snowshill and elsewhere was the mummers' play, performed every Christmas and featuring such characters as Father Christmas, King George, Beelzebub, the Doctor and John Vinney, a legendary strong man.

By the 1930s, the old way of life was rapidly disappearing. One of the early casualties was the village smithy, which following the retirement of the last blacksmith, was bought lock, stock and barrel by the American motor magnate, Henry Ford and shipped over the Atlantic, to be erected on his estate in Michigan, alongside other Cotswold buildings.

Snowshill Manor

Walkabout

1. From the car park, walk towards the village. Turn left at the Chipping Campden signpost and climb as far as a crossroads, commanded by a tall, multi-gabled and chimneyed house, standing in a terraced garden.

2. Turn right down into the centre of the village, with the church, standing in its irregular churchyard, on the right and wide views westward. The dominant crown of Oat Hill looms to the left.

3. Turn left to see the appealing southern approach to the village. Staddle stones, toadstool-like structures upon which hay ricks were once mounted to protect them from rats, have been incorporated into the wall on the right, a novel variation of use from the ubiquitous garden ornaments.

4. Retrace to the church. This is usually kept open, although the interior contains little of interest apart from some colourful kneelers and the font and Jacobean pulpit saved from the old church. In the churchyard, close by the chancel wall, is a well preserved double table-top tomb, with clear incised lettering on the ends and dated 1615.

5. Continue past the inn to reach the manor, also on the left. Apart from its collections, the building itself is well worth close inspection, as are the gardens. Do not miss the square stone dovecote, with its external stone staircase leading to the columbarium.

Weston-sub-Edge

Getting there:	Weston-sub-Edge lies on the B4632, 3 miles NE of Broadway and 2 miles NW of Chipping Campden.
Park:	As near as possible to the Seagrave Arms in the centre of the village (O.S. Landranger Sheet 150. GR 125412).
Introducing the village	Like its neighbour, Aston-sub-Edge, this village is aptly named, for it stands below the Cotswold escarpment on the fringe of the Vale of Evesham. Its buildings reflect its position between hill and vale, being a mixture of dark Cotswold stone and mellow brick, with a little timber framing included for good measure. It seems a pity that Weston stands astride a busy road, although its twisting main street at least has the effect of slowing down the traffic. Fortunately, the stretch of Ryknild Street passing close to the village has not been 'improved' as it has further north and although it is elevated from track status here, it remains merely an unclassified road.
Refreshments:	The Seagrave Arms.

A peep into the past

Weston-sub-Edge has plenty of history on the ground. It grew up alongside Roman Ryknild Street, on its way from its junction with the Fosse Way at Bourton-on-the-Water to Yorkshire and from medieval times until 1613 belonged to the Giffards, a wealthy and influential family, members of which held high office in church and state.

The site of the Giffards' manor house can be seen behind the church. Reduced now to a series of mounds and ditches, it must have been an impressive building and was surrounded by orchards, with a mill and fishponds close by.

The original parish church was possibly contemporary with the manor house but all that remains now is the 15th century tower, the rest being Victorian. Inside, however, is a huge 13th century stone altar and two carved stone figures, also medieval.

Among Weston's list of rectors was William Latimer, the Renaissance scholar who helped Erasmus to edit his Greek testament. A later rector was Canon G.D. Bourne, who was responsible for the enclosure of the open pasture of Dover's Hill, part of Weston parish and the scene of the annual Olympick Games. These had become such a nuisance by Victorian times, with up to 30,000 attending from far afield, 'merely for debauchery', that the Canon felt compelled to act. As a result, the Games were stopped and not revived until after the Second World War.

According to H.J. Massingham, writing in the 1930s, Weston-sub-Edge's position marked the dividing line between the 'Cotswolds proper' dialect and that of the Vale of Evesham. His observations were based on listening to the locals at the Seagrave Arms.

In Weston-sub-Edge

Walkabout

This includes a short stretch of field path which may be muddy after rain.

1. From the T-junction opposite the Seagrave Arms, walk along the B4632 towards Stratford. Immediately on the left and standing behind high walls, is Latimers, said to have been the family home of the scholar, with its diagonal chimneys and graceful finials.

2. Cross to follow the Dover's Hill signpost. The Hill, with Lynches Wood, makes an inviting backdrop. The fine cedar ahead stands by the manor house. This is 17th century, with mullioned and tran-

somed windows. A four-gabled and lanterned dovecote can be glimpsed in the grounds behind.

3. Beyond, Moat House is so named because of its position overlooking the moat of the old manor house. Further on, across the road, stands the converted village school. Notice the lion-headed drinking fountain, dated 1864, and the plaque recording the school's life – 1852-1985.

4. Enter the churchyard and after visiting the church, leave through a kissing gate at the far right-hand corner, The public footpath back to the village follows a line roughly parallel to the road and offers a clear view of the old manor site, together with the remains of the moat, indicated by old willows.

5. Veer to the left to go through a kissing gate. Cross a footbridge, noticing two ponds (former manor fishponds) over the hedge. Follow the right hand field margin and continue between gardens to reach a narrow road. Turn right, pass cottages and follow the path to the left to a road.

6. Turn left to reach the B4632. Go right along the pavement, passing some interesting houses. Beyond the rectory is Ryknild Cottage, with its distinctive arched doorway and gabled dormers. Manor Farm has a striking sundial with cherubs' heads.

7. Overlooking the corner at the end of the walk is a group of handsome stone houses and another with timber framing on a stone base and roofed with stone slates.

Willersey

Getting there:	Willersey lies on the B4632, 1½ miles NE of Broadway.
Park:	Village hall car park, signposted from Main Street. (O.S. Landranger Sheet 150. GR 106395)
Introducing the village	Few of the villages included in this book stand on busy roads, for the obvious reason that there is little joy in lingering along streets cluttered with noisy and air-polluting traffic. In the case of Willersey, however, its spacious greens, together with the right-angle bends at each end of the village street, serve to reduce the impact of passing vehicles to a minor irritation.
Despite being at the foot of the scarp, with Vale of Evesham villages as its near neighbours, Willersey's affinity lies without doubt with the Cotswolds. We have only to glance at the mellow stonework and fine proportions of the older houses along Main Street to confirm this impression. And anyway, the hills are only a glance away, providing Willersey with as enviable a setting as many an upland village.
Willersey is one of that fortunate band of villages that have attracted the attention of a gifted author. Algernon Gissing, brother of the celebrated Victorian novelist George, lived in the village for some time and in his book 'The Footpath Way in Gloucestershire', published in 1924, he devoted several chapters to Willersey and to its neighbour, Saintbury, thus providing us with a detailed impression of Cotswold village life in the first quarter of the century.
Refreshments:	Bell Inn. New Inn.

A peep into the past

Before the closing of the monasteries, Willersey belonged to the Abbey of Evesham. The abbots had a summer residence in the village and one, Zattan, designed the massive church tower.

In the 16th century, William Roper, son-in-law of Sir Thomas More, owned the manor, while in the next century the powerful Penderel family, were given their house by Charles II in gratitude for their help in his escape after the Battle of Worcester.

The annual wake was Willersey's great event until recent times. It was held on the green on Midsummer Day and attracted crowds from miles around. The weeks leading up to the wake were the most important time in the working year for the asparagus harvest was being gathered and everyone was busily tying the bundles of 'gras' with withy strands ready for market.

The pond on Willersey Green

Walkabout

1. From the car park, walk back to Main Street and turn left. Here, set behind the village pond stands Pool House, dating form the 17th century and reached between imposing stone pillars.

2. Cross Main Street to reach Church Street. At the junction stands a group of former barns, now converted into sumptuous homes – perhaps the "true old barn-houses grouped about the green like casual knots of worthies", admired by H.J. Massingham on his visit here in the early 1930s.

3. Church Street is both attractive and lively, with its post office/shop, hairdresser and school. The latter dates from 1844 and is still open.

The street ends at St Peter's Church. The churchyard offers delightful views eastwards to Saintbury and the Cotswold escarpment. The church itself, though revealing evidence of a blocked Norman south doorway and containing a tub font of the same period, dates chiefly from the 14th and 15th centuries. The fine tower, with its immense gargoyles sprouting from each corner, was built by the Abbey of Evesham but the beautiful vaulting inside is a good example of Victorian work. Fragments of medieval glass can be seen in the west window, depicting Mary Magdalene, an unknown saint, and two deer.

4. Retrace steps to Main Street and turn left. The first building reached is the ancient Bell Inn, known as the Blue Bell in Gissing's time and distinctive with its tall gables and chimneys as well as a bell turret over the porch. Follow the pavement uphill behind the garage to pass the Old Bakehouse. The pavement continues above the road as far as the junction of the Broadway and Chipping Campden roads, at which stands an attractive Methodist chapel converted from cottages in the 1920s.

5. The walkabout can be made into a circular by continuing along the B4362 as far as an unmarked public footpath on the right immediately before a row of cottages. Follow this to an estate road and turn right along it to reach another path on the right between houses. On reaching a T-junction of paths, turn right again back to the car park.

Those wishing to explore the footpath network around Willersey should buy a copy of the 'Country Walks around Willersey' booklet produced by the parish council and on sale in the village.

Winchcombe Area

The area based on Winchcombe, though comparatively small in extent, is one of sharply differing landscapes. The south west of the area features Cleeve Common, not only the largest expanse of unenclosed common in the Cotswolds but also the highest part of the region, rising to 326 metres (1080 feet) above sea level.

The countryside to the north west of the escarpment provides a striking contrast with the low-lying ground, relieved only by a few outlying hills, and drained by the little River Isbourne, flowing northwards from its source on Cleeve Common.

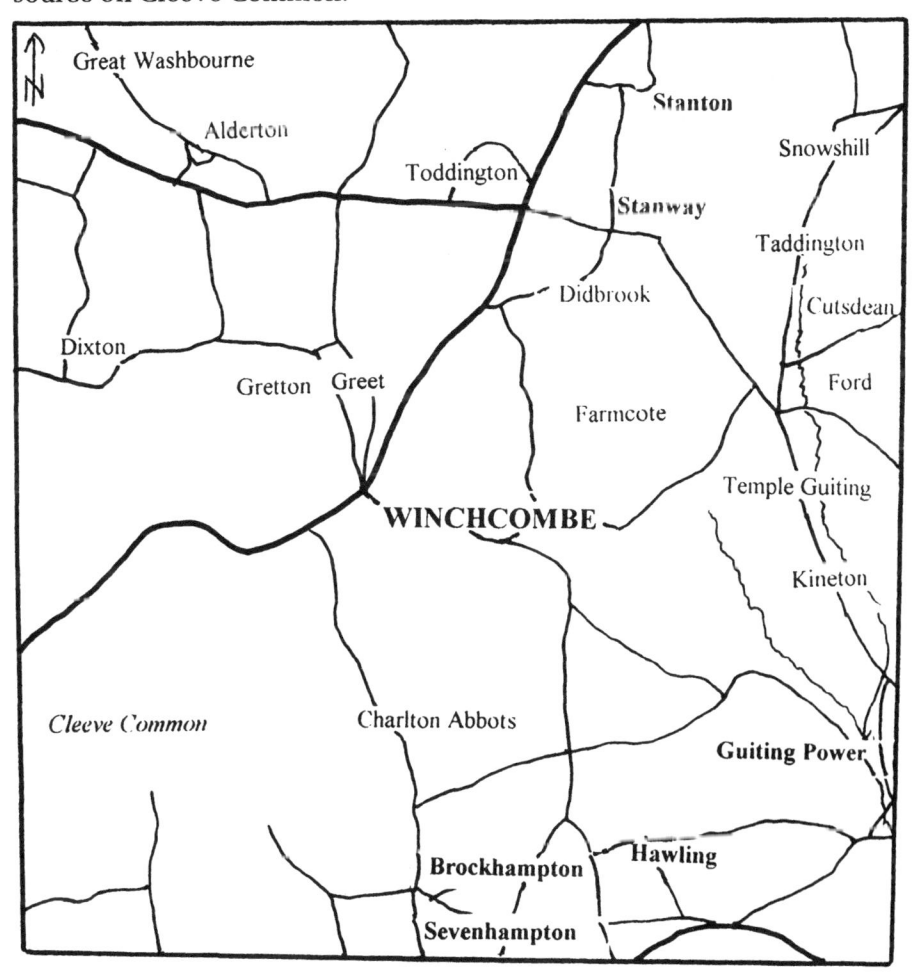

The villages in the area tend to be small and well scattered though many, such as Stanton, Stanway and Guiting Power, are of outstanding beauty.

Notable among the area's historic buildings open to the public is Sudeley Castle, on the edge of Winchcombe, famous for its associations with Henry VIII and the burial place of his sixth wife, Katherine Parr.

Nearby are the ruins of Hailes Abbey, a Cistercian abbey founded in 1245 and linked by the Cotswold Way long-distance footpath to Winchcombe. Stanway House and gardens offer seasonal public access while the Gloucestershire and Warwickshire Railway, based at Toddington, run steam trains to Winchcombe and beyond at weekends and during holiday periods.

Prehistoric sites within the area include Belas Knap chambered barrow, and camps on Cleeve Common and Nottingham Hill. Roman villa sites exist in Spoonley Wood and at Wadfield, both near Winchcombe.

The area offers fine walking, with sections of the Cotswold Way, the Wychavon Way and the Warden's Way, as well as numerous short circular walks.

Winchcombe

This small country town came to prominence in Saxon times, when King Offa established it as a regional capital of Mercia and founded a Benedictine abbey there. His son, Kenulf, father of the boy-king Kenelm, whose murder gave rise to a popular legend, extended Winchcombe's influence and by the 11th century the town had its own county for a short time.

Following the dissolution of the monasteries in 1538, Winchcombe Abbey was completely destroyed and the town's prosperity declined. Tobacco growing brought some revival in its fortunes in the 17th century but it was suppressed by the government to safeguard the Virginia monopoly.

Visitors to this fine historic town should not miss the 15th century 'wool' church, with its array of amazing gargoyles, the railway museum and the pottery.

Guiting Power

Getting there:	Guiting Power lies 1½ miles north of the B4068 and 5 miles SE of Winchcombe.
Park:	Village hall car park, reached along road past village stores. (O.S. Landranger Sheet 163. GR 095246).
Introducing the village	Grouped around two well-kept greens close by the confluence of the infant River Windrush and one of its delightful tributaries, Guiting Power is a good example of a Cotswold village in which a balance has been struck between preserving the old and beautiful while at the same time maintaining healthy community life. Despite the closure of its school, the village, through its amenity trust, is a lively place, with its own annual festival of music and art, staged in a spacious village hall. It also boasts two inns, a popular village shop, an environmental centre, and a network of well-used footpaths striking off to neighbouring Kineton, Barton and Naunton.
Refreshments:	Farmers Arms Inn. Hollow Bottom Inn.

A peep into the past

In 1902, the author Herbert Evans cycled into Guiting Power in search of material for his book 'Highways & Byways in Oxford and the Cotswolds.' What he discovered filled him with dismay: "Towards the close of the century, came the days of agricultural depression, and the church and village became partners in decay...The former presented a melancholy spectacle. The nave and transepts in their squalid deformed condition were alone used for service: for 15 years the chancel had been boarded off and was fast going to ruin. In recent years, the population has diminished by nearly one-half and some 30 cottages now stand untenanted and in various stages of dilapidation."

Fortunately, the desperately needed change in Guiting Power's fortunes was about to take place. The arrival of a new vicar heralded fresh hope. £2,600 was raised to repair the church and soon the village itself began to regain its vigour. The purchase of the manor by a new owner in 1958 set the seal on the recovery and since then Guiting Power has claimed its rightful place as a thriving Cotswold village.

The early 1990s saw the uncovering of some of Guiting Power's ancient past. Archaeological excavations in and around the present village unearthed evidence of extensive Iron Age remains – a fortified enclosure, pottery, a fertility object, animal bones – while to the north of the present church were discovered important Saxon remains, including the foundations of a tiny church.

These last discoveries may in time prove to be traces of the stronghold of Alwyn, a Saxon lord who resisted the Norman invasion and whose widow and property were given by William the Conqueror to one of his followers.

The first part of Guiting Power's name originates from the old English 'gyte', meaning an outpouring of water. Power is derived from the village's 13th century owners, the Le Poer family.

Guiting Power – village green and cross

Walkabout

1. From the lane by the car park can be seen the mound and stone-wall outline of the Saxon church. Follow the lane past the 16th century manor house and a group of barns to reach St Michael's Church, at the southern extremity of the village. Norman in origin, this was drastically restored in 1903 but fortunately its two original doorways were preserved, although that to the south was moved. Above the north doorway, notice the carved human head, complete with protruding tongue – an act of defiance, perhaps, directed at those critical of this much altered building?

2. Retrace steps to the car park and continue to the main street. The two greens are on the left. The first, overlooked by well restored cottages, features the medieval-style war memorial cross and a moving wall plaque to the wife of the former owner of the manor. Notice the phoenix fire mark above.

3. Proceed up to the second green. This is graced by a splendid horse chestnut tree, the lower branches of which almost hide from view the seat provided for those wishing to sit and reflect upon the restful scene.

4. Cross the road and follow the short path opposite to reach the lane leading from the village centre near the post office. By turning left along it, a pleasant walk can be taken to the lane end, and beyond along a footpath leading along a wooded valley and eventually down to a tiny footbridge leading to Castlett and Barton.

5. Retrace steps to the main street and turn left. Opposite the road to the church, another inviting lane, roughly parallel to that just walked, continues as a field-path to the attractive hamlet of Barton.

Hawling

Getting there: Hawling lies one mile north of the B4068 and 4 miles SE of Winchcombe.

Park: At the eastern end of the village, near the chapel by the road junction. (O.S. Landranger Sheet 163. GR 067231).

Introducing the village: Hawling is a tiny village, perched 900 feet above sea level in a vast landscape that was for centuries open sheepwalks. Despite lacking pub, shop and school, its wide views and appealing mixture of buildings, sheltered by a scatter of fine sycamores, beeches and horse chestnuts, lend it a certain charm.

A notice in the church porch makes sad reading. The threat of vandalism means that the building is open only at certain unspecified times. But at least the churchyard, with its array of interesting weather-worn tombstones, can be inspected at leisure and views of the Elizabethan manor house obtained from the public footpath leading from the churchyard south westwards to the Salt Way.

Refreshments: Craven Arms Inn, Brockhampton (2 miles west). Farmer's Arms and Hollow Bottom inns, Guiting Power (2 miles NE).

A peep into the past

As at Oddington and Little Rissington, the old village of Hawling was abandoned centuries ago in favour of the present site. And although the house platforms of the lost village are on private ground, they can be viewed from a distance on the walkabout.

Old Hawling stood alongside Campden Lane, an ancient road, now a bridleway, along which travellers and sheep flocks must have passed over the centuries. A little to the west is an even more important road, the Salt Way, along which that vital commodity was carried by teams of horses from the mines at Droitwich down to Lechlade on the infant River Thames, from which it was shipped to London.

An isolated farm a mile or so north of Hawling is all that remains of the village of Roel, which had withered away by the mid 15th century, possibly because of the spread of the great sheepwalks belonging to Winchcombe Abbey.

Hawling's open fields were enclosed in 1755 and the grid of smaller walled fields we see around the village today was created at that time. This was a period of great change at Hawling, as in the Cotswolds generally, and not only in agricultural practice. The new-found wealth the landowners led to the rebuilding of the church and the extending of the manor house with the adding of a new wing.

Since then, Hawling's fortunes have fluctuated. A period of population expansion in mid Victorian times caused a school to be built in 1860, well ahead of the introduction of compulsory education. However, numbers fell earlier this century and the school was closed. Some building has taken place in recent times but Hawling remains a small, isolated village, relatively untouched as yet by urbanisation.

Hawling village school

Walkabout

This consists simply of a stroll along the village street, with a short diversion along the one and only side lane for a distant but impressive view of the E-shaped front of the manor house.

1. Start from the tiny Wesleyan chapel, built in the year of Queen Victoria's accession, 1837. This serves as a reminder that nonconformity has a long history in the Cotswolds, John Wesley having spent much time in the area, especially at Stanton. Opposite the chapel is the rambling yet dignified Middle Farmhouse, dating from the late 18th century and recently renovated.

2. Along the street on the right is the former village school, with its 1860 datestone, and now serving as a village hall.
Oval windows are a feature of the barns belonging to the manor, and of the house itself. They suggest Georgian (i.e. 18th century) workmanship, when they were not only inserted in new buildings but also added in remodelled ones.

3. On the right on approaching the church is the old Rectory, parts of which are 17th century. Notice the elegant ball finials and the 1730 sundial over the entrance.

4. St Edward's Church was originally late Norman but was rebuilt in 1764, and restored a century later. The beautifully proportioned tower, with its fierce gargoyles and delicate pinnacles, is its best feature. Inside are memorial brasses to the Stratfords, lords of the manor in the 17th century.

5. Back at the start, after making the short diversion to see the manor house front, a view can be had of the medieval village, in a field to the right of Campden Lane as it climbs from the hollow. Those wishing to tackle a 2-mile circular walk, partly over fields, can do so by following Campden Lane a short distance uphill from the hollow to reach a waymarked footpath on the right. This leads to Hawling Lodge, from which the return route follows the lane which enters Hawling at the junction by the chapel.

Sevenhampton and Brockhampton

Getting there:	Sevenhampton and Brockhampton lie 2 miles north of the A40-A436 junction at Andoversford and 4 miles south of Winchcombe.
Park:	Near Sevenhampton church, reached from the unclassified Andoversford-Winchcombe road along a lane signposted 'Sevenhampton Church. No through road'. (O.S. Landranger Sheet 163. GR 033217).
Introducing the villages	These two tiny villages, half a mile apart, stand at the head of the valley of the River Coln, arguably the best loved of Cotswold rivers. With its source at 600 feet above sea level, the Coln has the highest rising point of all the Thames tributaries and flows prettily along its tiny intimate valley, fringed with waterside plants and happily remote from the bustle of modern life. Although Brockhampton – not to be confused with its namesake, a hamlet between Bishops Cleeve and Swindon Village – is the larger of the two villages and boasts a sumptuous former manor house (The Park) and a popular inn, Sevenhampton gives its name to the parish and lays claim to the Norman church that serves both villages.
Refreshments:	Craven Arms Inn. Brockhampton.

A peep into the past

A mystery surrounds Sevenhampton's origins. Large-scale maps show the site of a lost medieval village, known as Sennington, on a remote hillside half a mile to the west of the present village, yet the Sevenhampton we know today must date from pre-medieval times, for its church is a Norman foundation. Despite the similarity of their names, were they in fact separate villages, one wonders, and if so, why did Sennington wither and die?

Brockhampton Park, commanding the crossroads at the western edge of Brockhampton and now converted into flats, dates from 1639, although the greater part is Victorian Tudor. In 1788, its then owner played host to George III ('Farmer George'), who, having ridden over from his Cheltenham lodgings to visit Sudeley Castle, decided to extend his tour to Brockhampton Court to see a famous black stallion.

We are told that after inspecting the horse and stables, the king was invited to join the family for midday dinner, which consisted of Cotswold mutton followed by batter pudding. It is said that his majesty's appetite, sharpened by the bracing air, did ample justice to the humble fare and that he returned to Cheltenham in good spirits.

Sevenhampton ford

Walkabout

This is a longer-than-usual walkabout, of about 1.5 miles, almost half of which is along field paths, which can be muddy after rain.

1. Enter the churchyard. This contains a good collection of table tombs and the visitor is welcomed to the church by borders of flowers. St Andrew's dates from Norman times but it is to John Camber, a 15th century wool merchant from Worcester, that we are indebted for the fine central tower, supported inside by flying buttresses. Camber himself, who died in 1497, has as his memorial a modest brass on which he is depicted with fur-trimmed sleeves and a purse at his waist.

Overlooking the churchyard on the left is the elegant 16th century manor house, seat of the Lawrence family for over three centuries until they sold the estate in 1890. Sadly, the southern wing was destroyed by fire in the 1950s.

2. Leave the churchyard along the public footpath to the right of the church. This passes through a burial ground and enters fields through a kissing gate. The path passes through another gate close to Manor Farm, with its fine barn, and then follows the edge of a bank over a long field before dipping to a hand-gate. Beyond this, the path climbs to reach a lane leading into Brockhampton.

3. From the lane, a good view can be had of the buildings of the former brewery, dominated by a red-brick chimney. Brewing ceased in the 1930s but thankfully the inn alongside still thrives. Notice the ornate sundial on the row of the cottages opposite.

4. On reaching a road, turn right into the village. (Brockhampton Park is 0.25 miles to the left and can best be seen from the Winchcombe Road). From the crossroads at the tiny green, turn right along the narrow road back to Sevenhampton. Though somewhat bleak at first, this road eventually provides delightful views across the steep little valley. Notice the converted village school on the left.

5. Arriving at Lower Sevenhampton, it is worth continuing beyond the ford to the southern extremity of this attractive little village.

6. Back at the lane to the ford, follow the inviting waterside footpath signposted 'Brockhampton via St Andrew's Church'. This climbs eventually, via a stile and a kissing gate, back to the start.

Stanton

Getting there:	Stanton lies one mile east of the B4632, 3 miles SW of Broadway and 6 miles NE of Winchcombe.
Park:	Free car park along unclassified road (signposted Broadway) on NW edge of village. (O.S. Landranger Sheet 150. GR 068344).
Introducing the village	In any discussion on the loveliest villages in the Cotswolds, the name of Stanton is almost certain to be mentioned. Like its northerly neighbours, Laverton and Buckland, Stanton is essentially a single-street village and as that street peters out on the flank of the escarpment, it is spared the through traffic that blights so many Cotswold villages. That said, Stanton's charms are so widely known that the discerning visitor will try to avoid summer weekends and bank holidays, for although the worst trappings of tourism are totally absent, people-pressure at these times may detract from the pleasure of the walkabout.
Refreshments:	Mount Inn (at top of steep ascent at eastern limit of village street).

A peep into the past

It is difficult to appreciate, when gazing at the beautifully maintained houses lining Stanton's street, that in 1906, when Philip (later Sir Philip) Stott bought the manor and came to live at the Court, the village was in a state of decay. The wealthy Lancashire mill builder changed all that. By the time of his death, in 1937, he had transformed his adopted village into the place we admire today, carefully restoring the cottages and farms, bringing in modern amenities, and even filling gaps in the street with timber-framed barns, carefully dismantled and brought to Stanton from nearby villages.

Stott's caring influence also extended to the beautiful Norman church. Although a sympathetic restoration had been carried out during the Victorian period, Sir Philip employed Sir Ninian Comper, the foremost ecclesiastical designer of the time, to enrich the church with various features, among them a reredos, screen and stained glass.

Walkabout

1. From the car park, walk towards the village centre. Stanton Court can be glimpsed over the hedge on the left, while away to the right and forming a delightful background to the cricket ground, rises the great whaleback of Bredon Hill, with the twin wooded hills of Dumbleton and Alderton close by.

2. On reaching the junction with the main street, turn right into Manorway, the western extremity of the village, so named because it was the road to the original manor house. Dove Cottage, the first of three former timber-framed barns brought to the village by Sir Philip Stott, stands on the left, with a 17th century gabled dovecote behind.

3. The Manor, or Warren House, is a little further on to the right. It is a dignified building of two projecting gables linked by a crosswing and is believed to pre-date the inscription 'TW 1577' over the doorway.

4. Further along Manorway are the other thatched barns, now converted into private houses, brought from the Vale of Evesham. Retrace steps to the junction.

Stanton. The Village Cross

5. Opposite Stanton Court gateway is the Old Manor Farmhouse, with its decorated diagonal chimney stacks. Unusually, it has two date stones – 1615 on a gable and 1618 over a doorway.

6. Warren Farmhouse and Little Warrens are further examples of early 17th century Cotswold building – gables and mullioned windows displayed to good effect. Little Warrens, dated 1615, has heraldic glass in its windows.

7. Beyond the former village school, the street ends at Sheppey Corner, from which two lanes fork, that to the left leading to the Mount Inn and to the Guildhouse, that to the right climbing as the Cotswold Way footpath to the summit of Shenberrow Hill.

8. Retrace downhill to the village cross with its medieval base and shaft supporting a sundial and globe. The cross stands at the approach to St Michael's Church and the spire, one of the most elegant in the north Cotswolds makes an unforgettable picture. To the left of the distinctive two-storeyed porch another glimpse can be had of the Jacobean Court, former home of Sir Philip Stott.

9. The interior of the church reveals a Norman arcade, some old poppy-head pews, and two pulpits, one late medieval and the other Jacobean. It was from the latter that John Wesley preached on several occasions while staying at the rectory with the Rev. Kirkham and his family. Memorials worth searching for include those to such prominent families as the Izods, the Warrens and the Wynniatts.

Stanway

Getting there:	Stanway lies off the B4077, 1 mile east of its junction with B4362 and 4 miles NE of Winchcombe.
Park:	On the verge of the unclassified road signposted Didbrook, near the crossroads with the B4077. (O.S. Landranger sheet 150. GR 061322).
Introducing the village	Few villages throughout the length and breadth of England can boast a finer array of riches than this tiny place, nestling at the foot of the wooded Cotswold escarpment, the greater part of it set back from the Tewkesbury-Stow road. Indeed, many of Stanway's treasures need to be searched for and are therefore overlooked by most motorists, making it a perfect illustration of the late S.P.B. Mais's maxim: "Unless you go slowly, you will never see England at all."
Refreshments:	Old Bakehouse restaurant (on B4077). Mount Inn, Stanton (1.5 miles NE).

A peep into the past

Until the dissolution of the monasteries, the manor of Stanway belonged to Tewkesbury Abbey. The abbot had a fine house in the village and stored his grain in a vast 14th century tithe barn.

After the dissolution, the manor passed to the powerful Tracys, the last of whom married into the family of the Earl of Wemyss in 1771. The estate remains in the same family's hands to this day.

The Tracys owed much of their influence to their astute business dealings. They developed local quarries, had their own salt workings at Droitwich, and established paper milling by the stream above the village in what is still known as Papermill Valley.

A strange association with Stanway concerns Dr Thomas Dover, grandson of Robert Dover, who founded the so-called Olympick Games at Chipping Campden. The younger Dover, known as 'Quicksilver' on account of his having introduced mercury into medicine, was in his earlier years a ship's captain and is credited with rescuing Alexander Selkirk, (on whom Daniel Defoe based his Robinson Crusoe) from the island of Juan Fernandez in 1708. Dover's relationship with the Tracys is uncertain; however he was buried in the family's vault in St Peter's Church on his death in 1742.

Walkabout

1. Cross the B4077 and walk towards the centre of the village. On the right stands one of the most striking war memorials in the Cotswolds, a superb bronze depicting St George slaying the dragon, the work of Alexander Fisher with lettering by Eric Gill.

Stanway House gatehouse and church

2. As the road dips and veers to the left, a most distinctive building comes into view. This is the gatehouse of Stanway House, built about 1630 by a local master mason, Timothy Strong of Barrington, for the Tracy family and incorporating an incredible mix of styles – Gothic bays, Dutch gables and Renaissance gateway and chimneys – all fashioned in the rich golden local stone. Notice especially the scallop shell ornamentation, representing the heraldic device of the Tracys.

3. Enter the churchyard and walk to the right by the wall. From here a good view can be had of the west front of Stanway House, built for the Tracys in the 1580s on the site of the 'fair stone house' of the Abbot of Tewkesbury, with its vast 60-pane oriel window.

The northern section of the churchyard wall contains a stone coffin and other intriguing fragments of masonry removed from the church during its drastic restoration in 1896.

4. St Peter's Church, though outwardly perfectly in keeping with its delightful setting, suffered badly at the hands of its late Victorian restorers. Even so, its Jacobean pulpit is worth seeing, as is the modern altar, the work of the celebrated designer, Sir Ninian Comper.

5. Follow the road as it bends sharply to the right. Over the wall, also on the right, can be glimpsed the magnificent stone-roofed tithe barn, built for the Abbot of Tewkesbury in 1380. Another peep at this fine building can be had from the drive entrance to Stanway house further along the road.

6. Opposite the drive entrance, with its view of the House, its grounds and the tithe barn, stands a thatched cricket pavilion mounted on staddle stones, the gift to the village of Sir James Barrie, of Peter Pan fame. Sir James stayed frequently at Stanway House and captained his own cricket team, the Allahakbarries, in matches against local elevens.

A delightful two-mile circular walk can be taken from just beyond the cricket ground along a stretch of the Cotswold Way footpath, through Stanway Park to Stanton and back along the oak-lined country road.

Stow-on-the-Wold Area

The area of the north Cotswolds around Stow-on-the-Wold is exceptionally rich in attractive villages. A good number of these lie along river valleys, that of the Windrush, together with its tributaries, the Eye and the Dikler, in the west, and the Evenlode in the east. The latter takes its name from the village of Evenlode and forms the boundary separating Gloucestershire and Oxfordshire, as it flows between Bledington and Kingham.

As well as Stow itself, a scattering of villages stand on the higher ground between the river valleys. This wold landscape is strewn with the remains of prehistoric man – tumuli, barrows and hill-forts – although many of these have been ploughed out or otherwise almost eradicated.

There is also considerable evidence of Roman activity in the area. The Fosse Way (now the A429) sweeps through in a diagonal course on its way from Lincoln to Exeter, while Ryknild Street, which left the Fosse Way from Salmonsbury, near Bourton-on-the-Water, for Templeborough, Yorkshire, can still be traced as a rough track for two miles near Condicote.

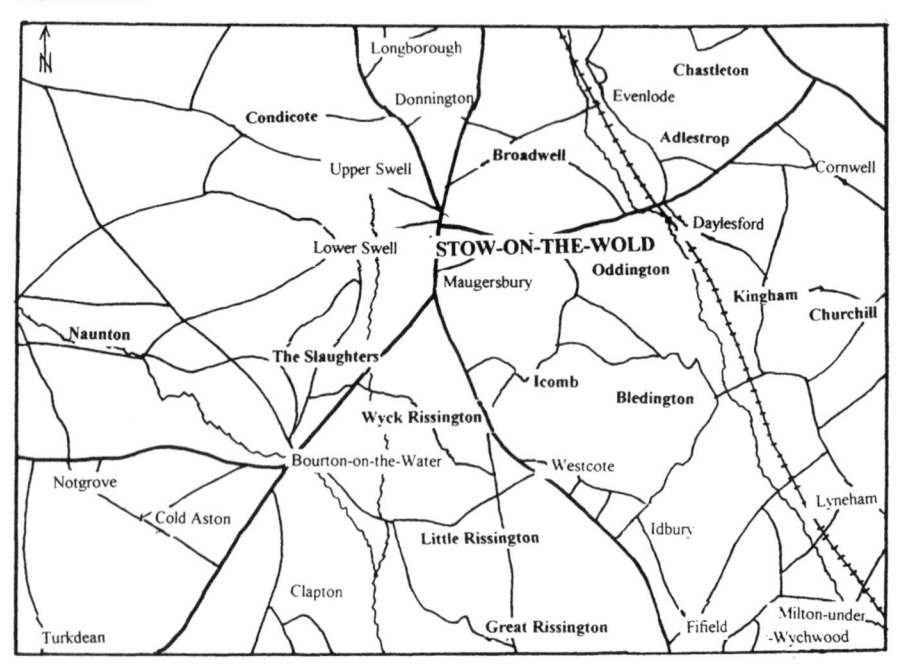

The largest village in the area is Bourton-on-the-Water which, together with Broadway, is the most popular tourist 'honeypot' in the entire Cotswolds. Its history dates back to the Iron Age, however, and its importance in Roman times has been confirmed by archaeological excavation.

The most notable great house in the area is Chastleton House, dating from the early 17th century and recently completely restored by the National Trust.

Literary associations include links with the clergyman diarist Francis Witts (Upper Slaughter), the founding of 'The Countryman' magazine by J.W. Robertson Scott (Idbury) and Edward Thomas's much-loved poem 'Adlestrop'.

Stow-on-the-Wold

Grouped engagingly around its ancient square, with its historic inns and distinctive shops and houses, Stow is the highest town in the Cotswolds and stands at the meeting of no less than seven important roads.

It owes its fame to its fairs, originally for sheep, and its horse fair is still a major attraction for miles around.

St Edward's Church, alongside the square, is of Norman foundation and is a notable landmark. Oliver Cromwell's victorious soldiers used it as a temporary prison for their Royalist captives after the battle in the town in 1646.

Adlestrop

Getting there: Adlestrop lies off the A436, 3 miles east of Stow-on-the-Wold.

Park: Village hall car park. (O.S. Landranger Sheet 163. GR 242272)

Introducing the village Here is a village that needs no introduction – to lovers of poetry and the English landscape at least. For when the express train on which Edward Thomas was travelling from Paddington to Ledbury stopped here without warning in 1914, he wrote a poem about it which begins:

> Yes. I remember Adlestrop –
> The name, because one afternoon
> Of heat the express train drew up there
> Unwontedly. It was late June.

Edward Thomas never saw the village he immortalised; he died in battle in 1917 but when the little station was unceremoniously lopped by Dr Beeching's axe in 1962, the locals salvaged the chocolate-and-cream Great Western Railway name board and erected it in a shelter at the entrance to their village, together with a platform bench bearing the poem on a brass plate.

How would Thomas, a lifelong walker, naturalist and keen observer of the rural scene, have responded to this little Evenlode valley village, close to the border with Oxfordshire? We can imagine his tall, lean frame striding along the meandering lanes from the station, his ever watchful eyes noticing the hedgerow birds – chaffinches, yellowhammers, thrushes – as he approached the village of mellow stone nestling beneath wooded Adlestrop Hill.

We can confidently assert that he would have liked what he saw, for Adlestrop has retained the warm stone, the colourful gardens and the quiet beauty that have appealed to its discoverers through the years.

Refreshments: The nearest pubs are the Fox and Horse and Groom, both at Oddington (one and a half miles SW) and the Fox at Broadwell (2 miles west).

A peep into the past

It seems that Adlestrop took its name from a Saxon named Tatel, who had a farmstead in this fertile spot a thousand or more years ago. The church of St Mary Magdalene, though dating from the 13th century, has been heavily restored. Even so, the memorials are well worth seeing, as several are to members of the Leigh family, with which Jane Austen was connected. One branch of the Leighs bought Adlestrop Park in 1553 and

The Post Office, Adlestrop

they later employed the architect Sanderson Miller and the landscape specialist Humphry Repton to improve their house and gardens.

The member of the family to which Jane Austen was related was the rector, Thomas Leigh. He was Jane's mother's cousin and the novelist and her mother stayed at the then rectory, now Adlestrop House, on at least three occasions early in the 19th century. It was on one of these visits that Thomas received news that he had inherited Stoneleigh Abbey, in Warwickshire, and the Austens accompanied him on his journey north to view his inheritance.

There has been considerable speculation as to whether Jane drew on her recollections of Adlestrop in writing her novels but conclusive evidence is lacking to support this.

According to the diarist the Rev. Francis Witts, of nearby Upper Slaughter, another member of the Leigh family, Chandos, was "an eccentric mortal", and a poet. Witts records that one of his compositions, entitled 'The Pleasures of Love', was "by the prudence of his friends suppressed." What outrageous work was the literary world deprived of in this way, we are left wondering.

Walkabout

1. From the car park, turn left. Pass a lane and the Adlestrop sign on the right and climb the hill as far as a lane to the village on the right.

2. Follow this lane into the village, swinging to the right by the snail topiary and then along a short diversion to the left to see the church, the former rectory (now Adlestrop House) and the old school alongside. Behind the church a glimpse can be had of the rear of Adlestrop Park. The lane to the right of the church is a public right of way and can be followed through the park to see the front of the house.

3. Retrace steps back to the junction and turn left by the post office – with its stone, brick, timber and thatch, surely one of the oddest in the country. Notice too, the phone, tucked neatly into a recess nearby.

4. Back at the start, a choice of footpath walks is on offer for those so minded. To assist with your choice, consult the map on display in the car park (and don't forget to pop a donation in the box before you leave).

Bledington

Getting there:	Bledington lies on the B4450, 4 miles SE of Stow-on-the-Wold.
Park:	By the pavement along Chapel Street, the no-through-road off the B4450, opposite the post office. (O.S. Landranger Sheet 163. GR 245228).
Introducing the village	Bledington, the most easterly village in Gloucestershire, is a spacious place, with many of its houses arranged round an extensive green. The River Evenlode, marking the boundary between Gloucestershire and Oxfordshire, flows close by, through low lush meadows, intersected by footpaths and the overgrown embankment of the former Kingham-to-Andoversford railway line.
	Although essentially Cotswold in character, red brick erupts unexpectedly around Bledington, a reminder that there was once a brickworks here. Fortunately, however, the legacy of this long-abandoned industry is more than offset by the high quality of the Cotswold stone buildings, some of which bear datestones from the early 18th century.
	Motorists driving through Bledington are advised to heed the 'Slow. Ducks crossing' sign, for these local inhabitants frequently emerge from their dabblings in the brook fringing the green to waddle across the road, or even to squat down in the middle of it if the mood so takes them.
Refreshments:	King's Head Inn.

A peep into the past

Bledington owes its name to its lowland situation by the River Evenlode, known as the Bladen in ancient times. It is recorded in the Domesday Book and its oldest feature, St Leonard's Church, dates back to the 12th century.

It is this church, standing at the south west corner of the village and overlooking a vast expanse of open country extending to the Stow-Burford ridge road, that is the village's chief claim to fame.

In the boom years of the wool trade, it belonged to Winchcombe Abbey and this prosperity led to its enlargement in the 15th century, when its tower was built, its nave heightened and its noble perpendicular windows filled with beautiful stained glass, said to have been the work of John Prudde, the glazier who worked in the Beauchamp Chapel at St Mary, Warwick. Puritan ravages and Victorian restoration made their impact yet St Leonard's remains an exceptional church, even on

Bledington Green

Cotswold standards. Open the old oak door, step inside and see for yourself.

Bledington's fortunes ebbed and flowed over the centuries. One visitor, cycling through the village in the early 1900s, described it as having 'the deserted melancholy air of one which has seen better days', attributing the cause to its low lying position which, he believed, deterred people from settling there.

Even so, the locals had a reputation for knowing how to enjoy themselves, excelling both at maypole and Morris dancing, epitomised by their celebrated dance, 'Bledington Hey Away'.

Bledington is one of that fortunate handful of Cotswold villages whose past has been comprehensively researched by a resident historian. In

1974, M.K. Ashby, a retired academic, and author of 'Joseph Ashby of Tysoe', published 'The Changing English Village', tracing the history of Bledington from 1066 until 1914.

Walkabout

1. From Chapel Street, walk towards the B4450 and cross straight over by the post office. Notice the old stamp vending machine, offering '2 ½d stamps for one penny'. Those were the days! As on Chapel Street, there are several examples of good Cotswold stone houses, with traditional mullioned windows, facing the green.

2. Turn left up Church Street. The stone slab fence on the left is one of a kind fairly common in the eastern Cotswolds, in which the stones are sometimes fastened together with metal brackets. Notice the 1741 datestone gracing the house on the left and the thatched roof nearby. Opposite is Manor Farm, dating originally from the 16th century and said to stand on the site of a rest-house built for the monks of Winchcombe Abbey.

3. Continue up to St Leonard's Church, which, together with the churchyard, is full of interest. The Oxfordshire Way long distance footpath passes the church on its way from the Evenlode Valley to its northern end at Bourton-on-the-Water.

4. To return to the start, retrace steps down Church Street for a short distance to reach a public footpath on the right, just beyond a thatched cottage. The path weaves between cottages and gardens to emerge via a covered way on the B4450 close to the post office.

Broadwell

Getting there:	Broadwell lies one mile east of the A429 (Fosse Way) and 2 miles NE of Stow-on-the-Wold.
Park:	As near as possible to the village green (O.S. Landranger Sheet 163. GR 204275).
Introducing the village	Give a village a spacious green, group Cotswold stone houses, cottages and an inn of varying age loosely around it. Result – a pleasant place for an on-foot exploration. Add to all this a gurgling little stream crossed by a ford, an ancient church standing amid a fine collection of 'wool' tombs and a tangle of tempting lanes and footpaths close at hand and you have Broadwell – one of the most alluring villages in the north Cotswolds, set comfortably away from main roads yet within easy reach of Stow-on-the-Wold and Moreton-in-Marsh. Allow plenty of time to explore this village. A leisurely look around will amply repay the effort and most likely prompt a return visit.
Refreshments:	The Fox Inn, Broadwell Green.

A peep into the past

The abundance of streams around Broadwell account for the settlement and for its name. These streams combine to form the brook crossed at the ford and upon which stood the village water mill close to the confluence of the brook with the River Evenlode.

St Paul's Church is Norman, with 13th century additions and a 15th century tower. The Victorians replaced the medieval windows of the nave and after removing a Norman door, built the semicircular tympanum into the wall of the tower stair.

There are fine monuments both inside the church and in the churchyard. Inside, look out for a tablet to Robert Hunckes, dated 1585, and for the alabaster effigies of Herbert Weston, his wife and child, kneeling at prayer and dated 1635. The outstanding collection of wool-bale tombs are of early 17th century origin and include one relating to the Chadwell family, depicting kneeling mourners on the side panels.

Like their neighbours, the Hodges, the Chadwells were prosperous sheep farmers and it was these two families in particular that accounted for much of the wealth in the area in Stuart times, and which is still to be seen in the form of handsome farmhouses with steeply pitched roofs, gabled fronts and mullioned windows.

The present green, restored for the benefit of the village by Lord Ashton

"Bale tombs" in Broadwell churchyard

of Hyde, a former resident, was formerly the common, on which the villagers grazed their stock and availed themselves of their traditional rights. It is referred to as No Man's Land in the Gloucestershire register of village greens and is one of the largest in the entire county.

Every village had its characters and Broadwell was no exception. Two in particular exerted their share of influence in Victorian times: one, a retired admiral, who lived at the manor, quarrelled with all and sundry and accused parish officials of among other things, trespass and embezzlement of funds. The other, a retired army captain and a veteran of Waterloo, who resided at Millbrook, alarmed his neighbours by staging noisy annual firework displays to commemorate the famous victory.

Walkabout

One short stretch of footpath may be muddy after rain.

1. From the Fox Inn, facing the green, turn right and follow the road as it skirts the green before swinging first left and then right to reach the junction with Chapel Street. Broadwell Farm, with its interesting group of outbuildings and dating from the 17th century, stands at the junction.

2. Walk as far along Chapel Street as is desired. The old bakery is on the right and the Baptist chapel is opposite a farm. Retrace steps to the junction.

3. Turn right. The house set back behind the wall is Millbank, built in the 17th century in traditional Cotswold style and enlarged by the famous architect Sir Guy Dawber in 1890. Continue to reach the green. The memorial stone to Lord Ashton of Hyde is on the left.

4. Cross the ford over the footbridge and climb past 18th century Rectory Farm on the left to reach St Paul's Church.

5. After seeing the church and the wool bale tombs in the churchyard, leave by the kissing gate at the southern corner and follow the public footpath. This crosses the drive to the manor house (visible on the right) before descending over a paddock to reach a hand-gate leading to a road. Keep straight on back to the start.

Chastleton

Getting there:	Chastleton lies 2 miles west of the A44-A436 junction and 5 miles NE of Stow-on-the-Wold.
Park:	Near the church. (O.S. Landranger Sheet 163. GR 249291).
Introducing the village	A tiny village on the northern tip of Oxfordshire, sandwiched between Gloucestershire and Warwickshire, Chastleton is best known for its magnificent manor house but deserves inclusion here for its quiet beauty and its alluring meandering ways.
Refreshments:	Cross Hands Inn (A44 – A436 junction) 2 miles east.

A peep into the past

Chastleton's oldest feature, a vast and almost circular Iron Age fort, stands well to the south east of the village and is accessible only to those on foot or on horseback.

The village as we know it came into existence in Saxon times. Norman remnants can be seen in the church and by about 1300 a manor house stood on the site of the present building.

By the 15th century, the Catesbys were lords of the manor and it was the last of this line to own Chastleton, Robert, later a Gunpowder Plot conspirator, who in 1602 sold the estate for £4,000 to pay off his debts and a fine imposed for his part in the Essex rebellion.

The purchaser was a wealthy Oxfordshire wool merchant, Walter Jones, who immediately set about building the fine manor house we see today, with five tall narrow gables flanked by staircase towers. Two rooms, in particular, are striking. The 72-metre long gallery, in which the ladies took their winter exercise and the great chamber, with its ceilings of ornate plasterwork.

It was in September 1651 that Chastleton House witnessed the kind of real-life drama that makes fiction appear commonplace. Arthur Jones, grandson of Walter and a fervent Royalist, had escaped after the Battle of Worcester and had ridden furiously back to Chastleton to hide from Cromwell's soldiers in a secret chamber. His pursuers, convinced that the exhausted horse they found in the stables was that of the fugitive Charles II, searched the house in vain and decided to stay overnight and to continue their search the next morning. As it happened, the room they chose was next to the squire's hiding place and it was only because his resourceful wife drugged her uninvited guests' wine that he was able to make good his escape.

The Jones family retained Chastleton until 1828, when it passed to a nephew, John Whitmore, who changed his name to Whitmore Jones. The last private owner, the widow of the Cambridge professor Alan Clutton Brock, lived in the house until 1992.

Walkabout

Chastleton's three most notable buildings are all in view from the churchyard gate – the church itself, the manor house alongside, and the dovecote standing in the field across the road.

1. The dovecote is an elegant stone-built structure, bearing the date 1762 and with an arcaded ground floor. The actual pigeon house was reached by ladder through a trapdoor. According to the excellent church guide, the field in which the dovecote stands, known as the Park, was the site of a house belonging to the prominent Greenwood family, which was demolished in the 19th century.

2. St Mary's Church, five centuries older than the present manor house, retains its Norman north doorway and characteristic arched pillars of the same period. Almost as old are the chancel and the font, while the 15th century glazed, fire earthed tiles are among the church's prized possessions.

Chastleton House and church

Protected by strips of carpet near the lectern are two brasses. One commemorates Katherine Throckmorton, grandmother of Robert Catesby, who died in 1592. The other is in memory of her son-in-law, Edmund Ansley, and dated 1613. Both brasses reveal interesting details of the attire worn by gentry of the period: Katherine and her five daughters wear caps and ruffs, while her five sons are clad in ruffs and cloaks. Edmund Ansley is depicted with his wife and ten children, including two boys in breeches and cloaks and two younger brothers dressed in frocks.

3. The manor house was in desperate need of restoration when it was acquired by the National Trust in 1992.

4. The short, sloping village street, dwarfed by the immense manor house, and shaded by giant beeches, sycamores and horse chestnuts, features some good stone houses, farms and cottages. On the right, a lane leads to Blue Row, a cluster of cottages, some thatched, renovated recently after years of neglect.

Churchill

Getting there:	Churchill lies on the B4450, 2.5 miles SW of Chipping Norton.
Park:	In centre of village, near the church. (O.S. Landranger Sheet 163. GR 284241).
Introducing the village	Churchill's pinnacled church tower is a landmark for miles around but the all-too-obvious assumption that the village was so called because of its church on the hill is, alas, somewhat wide of the mark. In fact the church we see today dates back only to the early 19th century, whereas what remains of its 13th century predecessor stands near the foot of the hill, as will be seen on the walkabout, together with the site of the old village, now but a few humps and hollows in a field. Modern Churchill, with its pub, village hall, garage, and houses of a mixture of limestone and ironstone, is clustered around the 'new' church. Some are roofed with thatch, several are 200 or more years old, and one bears a plaque proclaiming that it was the birthplace of Warren Hastings, the empire builder. Close by is a fitting memorial to Churchill's other famous son, William Smith, 'Father of British Geology.' Few villages can claim to be the birthplace of two eminent national figures, whose vastly different lives overlapped by almost half a century.
Refreshments:	The Chequers Inn.

A peep into the past

Until 1684, the village of Churchill clung to the lower slopes of the hill to the north west of the present village. In that year, a disastrous fire swept through the huddle of mainly timber-framed cottages, destroying virtually the entire settlement and leaving only the 13th century church intact.

With the passing of time, the village, by now constructed mainly of stone, began to re-establish itself higher up the hill. It was in one of these houses, in 1732, that Warren Hastings was born. The story goes that his childish hope was that one day he would become the owner of the Daylesford estate over the valley, which his family, having come upon lean times, had been forced to quit. That hope eventually became reality.

In the meantime, in a nearby cottage in 1769, was born William Smith, a tradesman's son who while attending the village school, became fascinated by fossils. Smith learned surveying as an apprentice at Stow-

Churchill fountain on the Green

on-the-Wold before being appointed first as engineer of the Somerset Coal Canal and then as engineer in charge of flood control in Norfolk. Later, he remedied leakage at Bath's hot springs and in 1801 published his 'The Natural Order of the Geological Strata of England and Wales' – the first treatise on British geology.

The Churchill of today extends from the old church to the new, with feelers reaching towards Chipping Norton, Kingham and Bledington. Fortunately, reminders of its eventful past are there for all to see.

Walkabout

Five roads meet near Churchill church, four of which lead to other villages. A good number of the most interesting houses stand alongside the B4450 as it heads towards Kingham Station and Bledington, though to see them involves the retracing of steps.

However, it is the fifth of these roads, a minor route leading to Kingham Hill and called Hastings Hill, that offers the most rewarding walk, despite again necessitating the retracing of steps.

To begin with the church. This was built in 1826 and was designed by an architect named Thomas Plowman, said to have been only nineteen at the time. It consists of a pick-and-mix of styles based on Oxford colleges – the tower on Magdalen, the walls on New College, and the internal roof on Christ Church Hall.

1. Facing the church, turn left. On the playing field on the right stands an arched and pinnacled fountain in memory of Charles Haughton Langston, a former village squire, who died in 1870.

2. Cross at the road junction to reach a tiny green, on which stands the rugged memorial to William Smith.

3. Turn left down Hastings Hill. Soon, on the right, is the birthplace of Warren Hastings, with its red plaque prominently displayed.

4. Continue down the hill to reach the churchyard, in which stands the chancel of the medieval church, reached through a gateway said to have been removed from the old manor house. The mounds and depressions in the adjoining field mark the site of the old village.

5. To extend the walk, continue along the road, which crosses the bed of the former Kingham – Chipping Norton railway line at Sarsden Halt, to reach Churchill Mill.

Condicote

Getting there: Condicote lies 1 mile north of the B4077 and 3 miles NW of Stow-on-the-Wold.

Park: By the walled green in the centre of the village (O.S. Landranger Sheet 163. GR 152283).

Introducing the village: No Cotswold village evokes the ancient past more intensely than does Condicote. High and away from it all on the wide, open wolds, it seldom attracts much attention from the guidebook writers. When they do condescend to mention it, their choice of adjectives tends to reflect their unease at discovering a village with an utter disregard for the picturesque: desolate, austere, strange, quiet – have all been employed in a vain attempt to sum up what it is that makes Condicote so different.

I first discovered Condicote when following in the steps of the Romans. I had tramped along Condicote Lane, part of the Roman Ryknild Street, from the south east and the village, crouching grey and bleak around its walled green seemed utterly remote, locked in its own time warp. No one stirred, not a sound broke the silence. I stood and stared, looked and lingered, and finally moved on, leaving the place to continue its slumber undisturbed. I still prefer to walk into Condicote along the old road, rather than drive there. You may care to try it for yourself.

Refreshments: Coach and Horses Inn, Ganborough (on A44) 2 miles NE.

A peep into the past

History abounds around Condicote. Prehistoric burial places – tumuli and a long barrow – are strewn over the landscape, while in the village itself are the scanty remains of a henge, a ceremonial monument almost 4,000 years old and the only one of its kind in Gloucestershire. Don't expect a Stonehenge – there isn't a stone in sight – but the telltale humps and hollows are there for all to see and indicate, to archaeologists at least, that they are part of a huge enclosure comprising a bank with a large ditch inside and a smaller one outside.

So was it mere chance that the Roman Ryknild Street, an important highway extending from the Fosse Way at Bourton-on-the-Water (or the Iron Age settlement of Salmonsbury to be precise), through middle England and eventually into Yorkshire, passed so close to Condicote's henge? Or was it that Ryknild Street, like so many Roman roads, was built along the line of a prehistoric track, possibly as old as the henge itself?

As the Ordnance Survey map shows, Condicote Lane poses other puzzles too. Why did the section through the village disappear, or for that matter, what became of the longer, final section from north east of Upper Slaughter to the Fosse Way (now the A429)?

But to return to Condicote. The village is recorded as Connicote in Domesday Book, a name said to have been derived from Cunda's cottage. two centuries or so later, the little church of St Nicholas was built. Thankfully, the Victorian restorers left us the original south doorway, with its rich ornamentation, and there are a few traces of 14th and 15th century work within.

The cross, too, dates from medieval times but its head is a replacement. It marked the boundary between the Slaughter and Kiftsgate hundreds, the old county sub-divisions, as well as having religious significance.

Condicote – the cross on The Green

Walkabout

Condicote Lane, now a roughly surfaced track, can be muddy after rain.

Stow-on-the-Wold Area

1. The best of Condicote is centred on its green, around which four good-looking farmhouses, the Norman church and the 14th century cross make an appealing group.

2. Three roads strike off from the green. That towards Hinchwick passes a mixture of old and new houses, beyond which a bridleway on the left can be followed for almost a mile, with sweeping views.

3. The road eastwards soon forks, with the left hand branch making for Longborough, via Luckley Farm, while that to the right heads for the Donnington Brewery and Upper Swell, in the valley of the tiny River Dikler. At the fork itself can be seen the humps and hollows of the henge referred to earlier.

4. But it is the road to the south, passing the cross, that offers the most rewarding walk. After leaving the village, this road, on the line of Ryknild Street, reaches a T-junction, opposite which an 'Unsuitable for motors' sign indicates that Condicote Lane, a two-mile stretch of Roman road, lies straight-as-a die ahead. Now we can walk in the steps of the legions, without fear of being mown down by petrol-driven chariots.

Great Rissington

Getting there:	Great Rissington lies 3 miles SE of Bourton-on-the-Water.
Park:	As near as possible to the green and the Lamb Inn. (O.S. Landranger Sheet 163. GR 200173).
Introducing the village	Much of Great Rissington, the southernmost of the three Rissingtons, is grouped pleasingly around a tiny sloping green. However, its most notable buildings – church, manor house and rectory – are at the foot of a slope in the south west corner of the village. As well as a tangle of lanes, the village is well served by footpaths and bridleways, by which it is linked with Little Rissington, Great Barrington, Sherborne and Windrush.
Refreshments:	The Lamb Inn.

A peep into the past

Despite its rather grand-sounding name, Great Rissington is a modest sized village well away from main roads. Like countless other villages it suffered badly during the years of agricultural depression and even as late as the early 1900s, its appearance, according to the author and traveller F.E. Green, was one of drab dereliction. Green records in his book 'The Tyranny of the Countryside' that he found Great Rissington looking 'as though the army of some conquering foreigner had invaded the Cotswold Hills and riddled the cottages with holes.'

He described rafters without thatch and windows boarded up. He was told by the rector that 20 cottages had fallen down during the time that he had held the living and met a labourer whose wage averaged less than 12 shillings a week and whose children lived chiefly on bread, lard and potatoes.

The gradual improvement in Great Rissington's fortunes as the century advanced was accompanied by profound change in the surrounding countryside. As the Second World War loomed, work began on the construction of a huge new airfield to the east of the village. This was to become the RAF Central Flying School, the main runway of which aligned directly with Great Rissington.

The base was for a time the home of the Red Arrows aerial display team, which attracted a steady stream of sightseers to watch their dramatic rehearsals from the perimeter fence.

Until its closure in the 1970s, the close proximity of the air base had

Stow-on-the-Wold Area

Great Rissington Church and Manor gates

a considerable impact on village life, providing work for its inhabitants but also subjecting the village to constant noise.

Since then, Great Rissington has settled into rural tranquillity. Its school and inn – it is the only one of the three Rissingtons to possess either – both flourish, its cricket ground on the brow of the hill above the village is well used during the summer months, and an increasing number of walkers ensure that the footpaths leading off in all directions from the village are kept open.

Walkabout

1. From the green, follow the signpost indicating the church. The route passes an interesting assortment of cottages, many old, arranged at various angles down the slope. There are good views ahead and away to the right across the Windrush Valley.

2. The Church of St John the Baptist dates from the 12th century and contains features added during the 14th and 15th centuries. Despite a drastic restoration in 1873, there is much of the old building to see, including a weathered stone panel depicting the Crucifixion in the porch and a delightful memorial to John Barnarde, who died in 1621 and "over whom Joane his wife put this monument. She also gave xx poundes stock for the pore here forever."

Even more touching is the memorial, complete with photographs, to the fallen of the First World War, including the 5 sons of Mrs W. Souls. The gabled manor house alongside is 17th century with later additions, while the rectory opposite, square and solid, is a good example of early 18th century style.

3. Retrace steps the short distance as far as a lane on the left. This winds blithely back to the Bourton road, passing yet more appealing cottages of varying age and a venerable farmhouse with spreading yews on either side of its entrance gate.

4. On reaching the Bourton road, follow it as far as a left hand bend by Lower Farmhouse. Turn right here up a lane, along which are some handsome old houses, including one with an elegant porch.

5. At the top of the lane, turn right by the former malthouse and follow the level road, with its wide views, back to the start.

Icomb

Getting there:	Icomb lies 1 mile east of the A424, 3 miles SE of Stow-on-the-Wold.
Park:	In the centre of the village, near the war memorial. (O.S. Landranger Sheet 163. GR 142227).
Introducing the village	Icomb is a small, attractive village nestling beneath the hill of the same name, overlooking the Evenlode Valley. It has no near neighbour, and is reached along quiet country roads, either from the Stow-Burford ridge road (A424) or, with many a twist and turn, from the B4450, between Stow-on-the Wold and Bledington.
	For those who prefer their village explorations to involve rather more exercise than a mere stroll, Icomb is sure to please, for its network of switchback lanes offers wide views across the Evenlode into Oxfordshire.
	Its neat cottages, well-tended gardens and general cared-for atmosphere are immediately apparent. It comes as no surprise, therefore, to discover that Icomb has made a habit of winning the Bledisloe Cup for Gloucestershire's best-kept small village – a sure sign that community spirit thrives in this quiet upland place, happily remote from the bustle of fast-track life.
Refreshments:	New Inn, Nether Westcote (3 miles SE). King's Head, Bledington (2½ miles east).

A peep into the past

Cotswold hilltops invariably bear traces of prehistoric settlement and Icomb Hill is no exception. The camp or fort indicated on maps is scarcely detectable to the inexperienced observer but we can take it for granted that the escarpment above the present village was inhabited upwards of 3,000 years ago.

Icomb's more recent history contains its share of oddities. Until 1844, the village, then called Church Icomb, was an 'island' of Worcestershire, isolated in the middle of Gloucestershire. To complicate matters even further, Icomb Place, the medieval home of the Blakets, was in Gloucestershire. Sir John Blaket fought alongside Henry V at Agincourt and his worn but impressive effigy, his feet resting on a headless dog, can be seen in the church.

Also to be found in the church is an account of the state of the building at the time of its restoration in 1871. It is hard for us to imagine, having seen the loving care with which the folk of Icomb maintain their village,

Icomb

that St Mary's then had mouldy walls, rotting timbers and a damp and filthy floor.

Sadly, the tower known as Guy's Folly, which had crowned Icomb Hill since 1805, was demolished in the 1970s and replaced by the present TV mast – 60 metres of stark uncompromising geometry visible for miles.

Walkabout

1. From the centre of the village, with the church on the left, turn right. Notice the old pump in the garden on the right. At the base of the chimney stack of the cottage opposite can be seen a rounded bread oven, a characteristic Cotswold feature.

2. The road soon bends to the right by two fine yews, opposite the drive to Icomb Place. The climb, though fairly steep on Cotswold standards, is rewarded by sweeping views to the south and east. A conveniently placed seat awaits by the road junction at the top of the slope.

3. Turn right. The road now descends to meet another road on the left by an old quarry planted with conifers. This road climbs Icomb Hill, swinging to the left to the TV mast, 800 feet above sea level. There are excellent views from here.

4. To return to the village, continue the descent to reach a fork in the road by the former school (dated 1874 and with its bell in the gable). The wide view eastwards is dominated by the tower of Churchill Church, beyond which can be seen Chipping Norton, at 750 feet the highest town in Oxfordshire. Turn right back to the start, passing some pleasing 17th and 18th century houses lining the village street.

5. Turn left by the Celtic Cross War Memorial to see the church. Its gabled saddleback tower is unusual, to say the least. H.J. Massingham called it morose, uncouth and devilish ugly; a trifle over the top, you may think. The churchyard is another good vantage point for views eastwards. Notice the tiny squint window in the church wall, through which the effigy of Sir John Blaket is visible. Inside the church, buy a copy of the excellent and inexpensive guide and take an informative look around. The Blaket tomb is the obvious *piece de resistance* but there are other notable sights, including the fine 13th century chancel and beautifully worked kneelers depicting local scenes.

Finally, read the gruesome story of the Dunsdon brothers, who used remote little Icomb as a hideaway while engaging in highway robbery in the 1780s and who paid dearly for their crime.

Kingham

Getting there: Kingham lies off the B4450, 4 miles SW of Chipping Norton and 5 miles SE of Stow-on-the-Wold.

Park: By the pavement on the wide stretch of Church Street. (OS Landranger Sheet 163. GR 258238).

Introducing the village: Kingham's name is best known for its railway station, a mile south from the village on the Paddington-Hereford line, and for Kingham Hill School, standing in extensive grounds high above the village in the opposite direction.

The village itself, though attractive and spacious, lies off the main routes and tends to be overlooked. It stands on the Oxfordshire bank of the River Evenlode, a tributary of the Thames, though the river, like the railway, is some distance from the village.

With its two main streets and large well-kept greens, Kingham is an ideal village to explore at leisure. It has a good range of stone buildings, some of greyish limestone, others of ironstone, and yet others of a mixture of the two. There is some thatched roofing and a few of the gardens are fenced with large stone slabs, attached with metal brackets, a feature also found in some nearby villages.

Refreshments: Mill Hotel. Plough Inn.

A peep into the past

Kingham is one of those fortunate villages whose history has been well researched and written about by several authors. An Oxford don, William Warde Fowler, built himself a house here and in 1913 wrote 'Kingham Old and New', a lovingly told history of the village along the lines of Gilbert White's great work on Selborne. Like White, Fowler was also an ornithologist and his best-selling book 'A Year with the Birds', first published in 1887, contains detailed accounts of the bird life in and around the village. Later, he discovered a breeding colony of the rare marsh warbler in an osier bed near the Evenlode and his painstaking observations of these birds, carried out between 1892 and 1906, placed him in the front rank of the ornithologists of his time.

Until its closure in the 1970s, Kingham was well known for its agricultural engineering firm, Lainchburys, manufacturers of threshing equipment. Ernest Lainchbury, a grandson of the founder, wrote 'Kingham, the Beloved Place' in praise of his native village.

Finally, in his recent book, 'The Rectors of Kingham', the Rev. R.N.

Mann describes an incident in the early 1850s when, during the building of the railway, Irish navvies lodging in the village caused annoyance to the then rector. Their ringleader, drunk and abusive, challenged the rector to a fight and was toppled from his perch on the rectory steps by the rector and his sons – with the aid of an oak hat-stand used as a battering ram.

Kingham's well on the Green

Walkabout

1. Walk into the village and turn left along Cozens Lane. This leads to West End. Turn right along West Street. Notice that many of the houses are built from tawny brown ironstone, while others have alternating bands of lighter grey limestone, known as oolite. On the left, on the roof of Manor Cottages, can be seen a rare medieval chimney pot. Continue as far as the crossroads. Notice the stone slab fence round the former forge on the right.

2. Cross straight over and walk across the spacious village green. Opposite the school, turn right and follow the access road to meet Church Street, opposite the Plough Inn. Notice the well, known as Stocks Well. The stocks themselves have long since disappeared and the fine old wych elm tree close by will soon be no more.

3. Continue along Church Street back to the start. Before leaving, notice the two fine houses on the same side as the church. The first, Old Rectory Cottage, was once the home of John Barrow, the eccentric son of a former Secretary to the Admiralty who retired to the village. Later, Freddy Grisewood, the famous broadcaster, lived here. His book of stories, entitled 'Our Bill', was based on Kingham and some of its characters. Next comes the handsome former rectory, dating from 1688. St Andrew's Church was heavily restored by the Victorians but contains one unusual feature – stone pew ends and backs, the work of a local mason.

Little Rissington

Getting there:	Little Rissington lies 1½ miles west of the A424 and 1½ miles east of Bourton-on-the-Water.
Park:	At the lower end of the village, near the start of the path leading to the church. (OS Landranger Sheet 163. GR 191198).
Introducing the village	Midway between Wyck and Great Rissington, Little Rissington clings to the hillside above the Windrush Valley, below the escarpment dividing this valley from that of the Evenlode, yet high enough to command sweeping views westward over the Vale of Bourton. It is a small, compact village, many of its cottages and farms lining the road from Bourton-on-the-Water to the A424, Stow-Burford road. This swings round two sharp bends as it gains height before attaining the bleak upland country above the village. It was through the building of a vast RAF base on this plateau shortly before the Second World War that Little Rissington's name became familiar throughout the country. The history of RAF Little Rissington is inextricably linked with that of the village itself and will feature in our peep into the past below.
Refreshments:	The Lamb Inn, Great Rissington (2½ miles south). Wide choice of inns, cafes and teashops at Bourton-on-the-Water (1½ miles west).

A peep into the past

For those who like their history spiced with a touch of mystery, Little Rissington is sure to appeal. As at Oddington, this is a village that for some reason seems to have abandoned its original site and moved uphill leaving its ancient church alone in the fields.

Historical records show that the old manor house, together with other properties, once stood near the church, but had disappeared by the late 17th century. Why? Plague, the scourge that swept through the country periodically in past centuries, seems the all-too-obvious reason for the desertion of Rissington Bassett, as the old village was called. But conclusive evidence is lacking. All there is to show is a humpy field and a network of lanes and paths. The rest is – mystery.

Two quaint traditions survived until recent times. One of these, the performing of children's singing games near the church, was revived in the 1960s by the Rev. Harry Cheales (see Wyck Rissington). The other tradition entailed the bridegroom lifting his bride over the church gate after their wedding, a custom also found elsewhere.

One of Little Rissington's wells

No visitor to St Peter's, Little Rissington, can fail to be moved by the two reminders of the village's association with the RAF Central Flying School. Inside the simple restored Norman church is a window to the young men, including members of the Red Arrows aerial display team, who died while serving at the base. In the churchyard can be seen rows of gravestones, all in Portland stone, of these men, who trained and flew in these Cotswold skies before giving their lives in the service of their country.

RAF Little Rissington is no more but through these graves its memory will remain green to all who visit this solitary little church.

Walkabout

1. From the lower end of the village, by the church path, walk along the pavement which, after passing cottages and a bridleway to Wyck Rissington, climbs with the road to the right. There are some good-looking houses fronting the road. Notice also the former water supply outlet, suitably dated and bearing the initials of the benefactor who installed it. Further on, on the right, is the former school, dated 1840, showing that education for the village children began 30 years before compulsory schooling became law.

2. At the sharp left hand bend, turn right down Pound Lane, so named after the enclosure, long gone, in which stray livestock were impounded. The lane soon swings to the right, leaving modern houses behind. On the left are Manor Cottages, converted from a farmhouse built in the 17th century and chosen by the famous architect Sir Guy Dawber as an example of Cotswold building at its best. Notice a second water outlet on the opposite side of the road.

3. Cross the main street and walk down the path and across a field to the church. After seeing the churchyard and the interior of the building, follow the path to the left of the doorway and go through the kissing gate for an impressive view of the Vale of Bourton, with its lakes formed from old gravel pits in the 1970s.

Naunton

Getting there:	Naunton lies half a mile north of the B4068, 5 miles west of Stow-on-the-Wold.
Park:	Near the church, at the western end of the village. (O.S. Landranger Sheet 163. GR 113233).
Introducing the village	One of the most photographed villages from afar in the Cotswolds, Naunton straggles for almost a mile along the upper reaches of the River Windrush. Yet of the countless number of camera-brandishing admirers that capture it on film from the high road (B4068) between Andoversford and Stow-on-the-Wold, very few take the trouble to discover its charms at close quarters. And Naunton's charms are many. At its west end, St Andrew's Church stands close by the Windrush, while a group of splendid beeches spread their canopy over a handsome cluster of neighbouring buildings, one of which, Littons, boasts an upper traceried window that would grace any church. The walkabout reveals many more fine Cotswold buildings, some dating from the 17th century, and the river, flowing fast and clear beneath its bridges, enhances the return journey.
Refreshments:	Black Horse Inn.

A peep into the past

The collections of sea urchins, ammonites and brachiopods displayed in gardens and on window sills in Naunton serve as a reminder that the village has a long history of quarrying. Naunton's speciality was in fact stone roofing slates, of which up to 30,000 a week were once produced from thin seams twenty metres deep by a labour force of over 100 men. Many of these high quality slates were transported considerable distances; for instance, Naunton roofs feature on many of the Oxford colleges.

The oldest surviving man-made feature can be seen in St Andrews Church. This is a tiny Saxon cross, found when the porch was being built in 1878 and now displayed high in the west wall. St Andrew's itself dates from the 12th century, and there is evidence of 15th, 16th and 19th century work. Not to be missed are the finely carved white stone pulpit of about 1400 and a number of intriguing monuments, including a marble tablet near the altar to Ambrose Oldys of Harford, on which it is recorded that his father was 'barbarously murthered by ye rebells' in 1645. Nearby is a brass plate to Clement Barksdale, author of 'A Cotswold Muse', who died at Naunton in 1687 after having been a vicar at Hereford, chaplain at Sudeley Castle during the Civil War, and a teacher at Hawling before ending his days as Rector of Naunton.

Apart from the church, Naunton's two oldest buildings, both dating from about 1600, are Cromwell House, at the eastern end of the village, and the dovecote. Cromwell House is said to have got its name from the Aylworth family, one time owners, who were stout supporters of the Lord Protector. One of the Aylworths, Richard, figured prominently in the Battle of Stow in 1644. Externally, it has changed little with the passing of time and is perhaps the most striking house in the village.

The much-photographed dovecote, seen towards the end of the walkabout, is a good example of the traditional four-gabled Cotswold type with a central turret.

To the south of Naunton and separated from it by the ridge road

Naunton from the hills

(B4068), are Aylworth and Lower Harford, both of which are lost medieval villages, surviving only as isolated farms.

Walkabout

The short stretch of footpath may be muddy after rain.

1. From the church, walk into the village, crossing the Windrush over Parson's Bridge, so called because it was built by the Rev. John Hurd, rector of the village, in 1819, replacing stepping stones.

2. Turn right at the junction and climb the slope. The buildings on the right, apart from the Victorian Baptist Chapel, present their backs to the road, their fronts facing south across the valley.

3. Continue down the main street and then up the lane on the left, just before the inn, to see the old workshop on the right, with its collection of fossils, beyond which, standing back from the road, is an old barn fashioned from huge rough beams set at a gravity-defying angle.

4. Back on the main street, continue beyond the inn to see Cromwell House, on the left, and at the end of the village, the former 17th century water mill on the right, one of several corn mills along the Windrush.

5. Retrace as far as the bridge on the left, opposite the lane walked earlier. Cross and turn right along the riverside footpath (later surfaced) which is followed back to the start and which passes the dovecote.

Oddington

Getting there:	Oddington lies off the A436, 2½ miles east of Stow-on-the-Wold.
Park:	Lower Oddington. By the pavement near the church and the village hall. (OS Landranger Sheet 163. GR 229259).
Introducing the village	Oddington is a long village, straggling for almost a mile over the lower wolds between Stow and the River Evenlode. Hardly surprisingly, it is divided into two parts, Upper to the west and Lower to the east but as houses and farms are strung out along the road, there is no distinct break between the two.
Three roads connect Oddington with the A436 and another with the B4450. Walkers can travel by field-paths in every direction, with especially tempting walks to Broadwell, Daylesford and Bledington. A quarter of a mile eastwards along the A436 from Lower Oddington lane end is the site of Adlestrop railway station, a victim of the Beeching axe in the early 1960s but immortalised in the poem by Edward Thomas. (See Adlestrop Village).
Refreshments:	Horse and Groom Inn, Upper Oddington. Fox Inn, Lower Oddington.

A peep into the past

There was an Oddington in Saxon times. It stood to the south of the present Lower Oddington but it had been abandoned by the early 18th century, leaving the Church of St Nicholas alone under the trees by the bridleway to Bledington.

So although in one sense, old Oddington is a 'lost' village, instead of allowing its name to disappear altogether, the villagers simply moved up to higher, drier ground. Why? We simply don't know. Some would have us believe the plague was the reason but there is no proof that this was so. All we know is that the village that had once boasted a residence of the Archbishop of York and which had been visited by Henry III, was deserted and in time disappeared.

Until the church of the Holy Ascension was built in 1852, the villagers continued to worship in their Norman church. After that date, however, St Nicholas's was left to its fate and although burials still took place in the churchyard, the building became so neglected that a vixen is said to have reared her cubs in the pulpit.

It was not until the Rev. Hodson became rector in 1912 that the long and difficult task of restoring the old church began. As can be seen on

Church of St Nicholas: Jacobean pulpit

the walkabout, we owe the restorers a tremendous debt, for this wonderful building now enriches the lives of villagers and visitors alike.

Walkabout

As with all linear villages included in this book, some retracing of steps is unavoidable. In the case of Oddington, this is a distinct advantage, for there is so much of interest to see that something missed the first time can be seen on the return.

1. Facing the village hall, turn right along Lower Oddington village street. The first of several fine old houses is soon reached on the left. This is the Manor House, beautifully proportioned and set at an angle to the road.

2. Pass the lane on the right leading to St Nicholas's Church. Immediately beyond, also on the right, notice the ornate 1728 date stone on the Old Post Office. Three elegant houses, all on the right, come next. First, standing back from the road, is Rectory Farmhouse, dating from the 17th century. Beyond can be seen the Old Rectory, also 17th century. Close by stands Oddington House, even older in origin but remodelled and extended early in the 19th century.

3. On reaching the Fox Inn, retrace as far as the lane down to St Nicholas's Church. This passes a house on the left recently converted from a derelict Cotswold barn before climbing gently to reach the church. This is packed with good things. Do not miss the beautiful Jacobean pulpit. The story of its use by a vixen is engagingly illustrated on one of the colourful hassocks nearby. The huge Doom wall painting repays close inspection – what terror it must have struck into the hearts of simple village folk!

4. Retrace steps to the car. Those wishing to see the rest of the village should continue along the winding road, which eventually dips to a small green. The no-through-road on the left is well worth a short diversion, as it leads to three distinctive old houses hidden from the road.

5. Upper Oddington, with its cluster of ironstone cottages, is not far away and refreshments at its friendly pub should make the return walk even more pleasant.

The Slaughters

Getting there:	Upper and Lower Slaughter lie between the A429 and B4068, 2½ miles and 1½ miles north of Bourton-on-the-Water.
Park:	Upper Slaughter: Square near church (O.S. Landranger Sheet 163. GR 156232). Lower Slaughter: by riverside at entrance to village from A429. (O.S. Landranger Sheet 163. GR 166225).
Introducing the villages	Less than a mile apart, Upper and Lower Slaughter are linked by a delightful riverside footpath as well as by a meandering unclassified road. Many visitors park at one and walk to the other, a strongly recommended method of exploration. The name Slaughter conjures up bloodthirsty images totally unrelated to fact. It was most likely derived from a German word for wet, uneven ground, or possibly from an early English spelling of sloe tree. Take your pick but ignore the gore! The Slaughters are lovely Cotswold villages in the valley of the tiny River Eye, or Slaughter Brook, but there the resemblance ends. Upper Slaughter, the larger of the two, is grouped around a small square, with its church alongside and evidence of the motte and bailey of a castle commanding the slope above the tiny valley. Lower Slaughter, by contrast, is essentially a double row of impeccably maintained cottages on either bank of the Eye, which is spanned by miniature footbridges connecting the car-free village street and green with the unclassified road between the A429 and Upper Slaughter.
Refreshments:	There are no pubs in the Slaughters, only hotels. Bourton-on-the-Water offers a choice of pubs, cafes and teashops.

A peep into the past

The site of Upper Slaughter's Norman castle is virtually undetectable and we can only admire the Tudor manor house, one of the finest in the Cotswolds, at a distance through its ornamental gates. But we can discover a great deal about the more recent past of the village and its surrounding area from 'The Diary of a Cotswold Parson', kept by the Rev. Francis Witts between 1820 and 1852. Witts was a man of many parts – rector, magistrate, horseman, and later, lord of the manor of Upper Slaughter – and on his death, a vast mortuary chapel was created in the church, paid for by public subscription. The Lords of the Manor Hotel, with its spacious grounds and lake, once the rector's home, can be seen from the field path to Lower Slaughter.

Lower Slaughter's manor house was built by Valentine Strong of Barrington, one of a distinguished family of master masons, who worked on the rebuilding of St Paul's Cathedral after the Great Fire. It was the seat of the Whitmore family from 1611 until 1964.

The watermill (now a museum) dates from the early 19th century and was still working until the Second World War. The overshot wheel was driven by water from the River Eye by means of a leat built sufficiently high above the river to provide the necessary power. Although no longer functioning, its simple yet effective method of working can still provide an absorbing topic for discussion with children.

Upper Slaughter ford

Lower Slaughter mill

Walkabout

Upper Slaughter

1. From the square, take the road shown as 'Unsuitable for motors', to the right of the church. Notice the cottages on the left, which were remodelled by Sir Edwin Lutyens in 1906 in the local style. Beyond the old school (datestone 1846) descend the bank by a magnificent sycamore tree to the right of the two tiny footbridges spanning the River Eye.

2. Turn right along the lane. At the T-junction, turn right again to return to the start, passing the riverside footpath to Lower Slaughter on the left.

3. To extend the walkabout to include the Manor House, cross the road from the square and take the other no-through-road. At its end, follow the footpath on the right between walls. The manor gates are to the left at the end.

Don't forget to visit the church, if only to see the Witts mortuary chapel.

Lower Slaughter

Depending on the direction from which it is approached, the main features to see are the Manor House, with its stabling and splendid dovecote, and the watermill, which despite its out-of-place red brick chimney, is one of the most photographed buildings in the Cotswolds.

Whatever the time of year you choose to visit Lower Slaughter, you'll never walk alone.

Wyck Rissington

Getting there:	Wyck Rissington lies between the A429 and the A424, 1½ miles NE of Bourton-on-the-Water.
Park:	By the pavement near the church. (OS Landranger Sheet 163, GR 192215).
Introducing the village	The most northerly of the three Rissingtons and to many the most appealing, Wyck Rissington is a tiny village scattered haphazardly around a large and delightful green. The more straightforward of the two approaches is from the A429, between Bourton-on-the-Water and Stow-on-the-Wold, but the less direct way – from the Stow-Burford road (A424) – is far more impressive. This way involves descending a single-track road from Wyck Beacon, a prehistoric round barrow on the summit of the ridge dividing the Evenlode and Windrush Valleys. The narrow road twists and turns down to the village, its stumpy church tower beckoning over the hedges.
It is difficult to realise, while wandering along the quiet village street and over the vast green, that this sleepy little place has as its near neighbour Bourton-on-the-Water, the honeypot of the Cotswolds, with its milling crowds and rampant commercialism. For here, in abundance, are space and peace, two precious commodities that become scarcer with the passing of time.
Refreshments:	There is a wide choice of inns and teashops at Bourton-on-the-Water.

A peep into the past

Wyck Beacon prehistoric burial mound is evidence that this area was inhabited at the dawning of history. Later, Iron Age people built a camp at Salmonsbury nearby and then the Romans swept their Fosse Way over the tiny River Dikler a mile to the north.

But Wyck Rissington's oldest surviving building is the church of St Laurence, rebuilt in the 13th century. It has much of interest, especially the windows in the chancel, and there are some unusual wooden plaques depicting the life of Christ, said to be Flemish and about 400 years old.

Two remarkable men of our own century are commemorated in this beautifully maintained church. On the organ is a plaque to the composer Gustav Holst, whose first professional appointment was as organist here. The other is a memorial in the wall of the nave to Canon Harry Cheales, a well-loved rector who, after a vivid dream, built a maze in his garden, based on the pre-Reformation belief that life could be interpreted in the

Wyck Rissington green

form of a winding pathway, with guidance points to help pilgrims along the way. The maze has now gone but appropriately, the Canon's memorial is a stone representation of his handiwork.

Walkabout

1. Wyck Rissington being a single-street village, the walkabout consists merely of a stroll from the church to the northern limit, beyond the end of the green. This is pleasurable enough in itself, but with the fringe of horse chestnut trees, the Victorian drinking fountain, the pond by College Farm, with its resident ducks and skulking moorhens, and the subtly different yet uniformly attractive houses, there is plenty to enjoy.

2. The houses strewn around the green, farmhouses and cottages, are chiefly 17th and 18th century, built of local Cotswold stone and mostly with matching stone-tiled roofs. The exceptions are two rows

of cottages, one group of which has red-tiled roofs. These are 19th century additions to the village, which otherwise has changed little with the centuries.

3. Wyck Rissington is the last village along the Oxfordshire Way, a 66-mile long-distance footpath extending from Henley-on-Thames to Bourton-on-the-Water. The route descends from Wyck Beacon through the churchyard and after passing through the village, strikes off to the left along a bridleway towards the alluring little River Dikler. This stretch of water meadows is now a nature reserve and makes a worthwhile extension to the walkabout for those with energy to spare.

4. Walking back over the green, one wonders whether the 17-year-old Gustav Holst, on his way to play the organ at the little church a century ago, found inspiration here. We know he did so at Cranham, another Cotswold village he was to discover later, for he named a hymn tune in its memory. It too, has a wide green, with a church at its far corner, but is a more rugged place altogether than this tranquil spot, sheltering beneath Wyck Beacon in the valley of the Dikler.

Northleach Area

The area of the Cotswolds centred on the little town of Northleach in many ways typifies the general perception of the region. It is predominantly rolling wold country that was for centuries open sheepwalks, which after its enclosure with drystone walls became largely arable farmland.

The upper reaches of two delightful rivers, the Coln and the Leach, have carved their gentle valleys into this upland scene and a few of the area's villages, such as Withington, Coln St Dennis and Eastington have become established in the sheltered situations they offer.

By contrast, other villages, such as Clapton, Notgrove and Cold Aston, are perched high on the open wold and have more than a passing resemblance to the villages of the Pennines and other upland regions.

Two important roads meet in the middle of the area. The Roman Fosse Way descends steeply (on Cotswold standards) to cross the Coln at Fossebridge before sweeping north eastwards towards Stow, while the A40 carries speeding traffic between Burford and Cheltenham.

Near Chedworth, one of the larger villages in the area, are the remains of a superbly restored Roman villa, in a delightful woodland setting, the property of the National Trust.

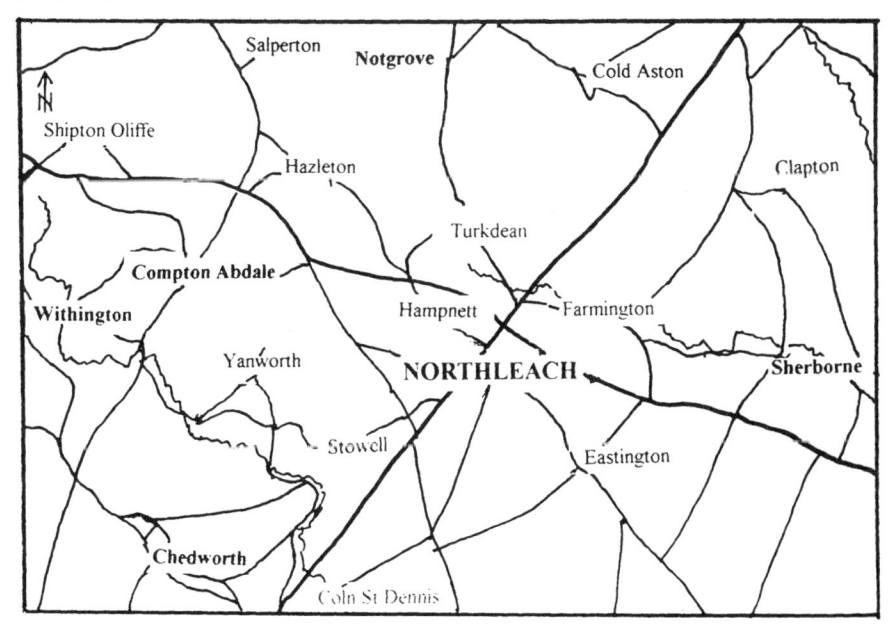

The Trust also owns the Sherborne estate on the eastern edge of the area. Among its recent initiatives in the interests of nature conservation is the restoring of the former drainage system on the land bordering the Sherborne Brook.

Northleach

Since it was bypassed by the A40 in the 1980s, Northleach has reverted to the quiet backwater status it enjoyed before the age of the supremacy of the car. The town was built around a triangular market place in the 13th century and its graceful buildings reflect the prosperity it acquired through the wool trade.

Further evidence of this is provided within the magnificent parish church overlooking the market place, which contains memorial brasses to the town's 15th century wool merchants, the Midwinters, the Forteys and the Bushes, who established Northleach as a prominent wool centre and whose bequests enriched their church. They are depicted in the dress of the period, often complete with purse, and with feet resting on lifelike representations of the sheep to which they owed their wealth.

At the west end of the town, housed in a former late 18th century prison, is the Cotswold Countryside Collection, a museum of rural life and agricultural history.

Chedworth

Getting there:	Chedworth village is 4 miles SW of Northleach. Easiest approach is from A429 south of Northleach.
Park:	By or near the church. (OS Landranger sheet 163. GR 052122).
Introducing the village	To many visitors, Chedworth means a Roman villa, maintained by the National Trust and one of the finest historical relics in the Cotswolds. Chedworth is in fact a village, and to complicate matters, village and villa, though only a mile apart by footpath, are separated by almost 4 miles of winding lanes. The villa's attractions need no further praise here; we are concerned with the village from which it takes its name. Chedworth stands high, above a tiny tributary stream of the River Coln. It is a large village by Cotswold standards and straggles for almost a mile along the west bank of the miniature valley. Until the 1960s, a railway wriggled its picturesque way through Chedworth, linking Andoversford Junction with Cirencester. All that remains are blue brick walls that once supported bridges, and cuttings and embankments now serving as wildlife havens.
Refreshments:	The Seven Tuns Inn.

A peep into the past

Chedworth prospered during the boom years of the Cotswold wool trade, when its manor house was built and its Norman church extended by the powerful Beauchamps, one of whom, Anne, married Richard Neville, Earl of Warwick, the famous Kingmaker.

Chedworth's great event took place in 1491, when Henry VII's queen, Elizabeth of York, visited to inspect the completed church extensions. The main street, Queen Street, was named in her honour. The church's fine tall windows remain to this day, together with carved heads of the King and Queen and other contemporary figures. Visit the church, buy the excellent guide, and seek out these, and the many other intriguing features at the end of your walkabout.

Walkabout

This is at the northern end of the village, where church, manor and inn are grouped close together.

1. From the church, walk back towards the road junction. In doing so,

Chedworth from the Seven Tuns Inn

peep over the wall on the right to see the manor house and its gardens. These include an ornamental pond from which water rushes down towards the Seven Tuns Inn. Notice the distinctive barn in the grounds. Its elegant, though out-of-place window came from Cheltenham College, whereas the doveholes in the gable are traditionally Cotswold.

2. From the junction, take the Lower Chedworth road, passing some appealing houses with original stone-tiled roofs. Turn right at the Calmsden road, then left by Smuggs Barn Cottage.

3. From the old railway bridge, there is a glimpse of the overgrown track bed. Keep on past the school down to a T-Junction by Hawks Lane

House. Turn left. There are good views now across the little valley, with paths leading to scattered farms and cottages. Notice the old chapel on the left, now the headquarters of the Chedworth Silver Band, founded in mid-Victorian times. On the left, beyond the site of the railway bridge, is mullioned and gabled Cromwell House, dating from about 1600.

Back at the Calmsden turn, retrace steps to the junction, where a choice of two benches offer a rest, complete with a view down Queen Street. This is our next objective, with the Seven Tuns (dated 1610) handily situated for refreshment and with a mini water wheel opposite. A short way down the slope, notice a Victorian letterbox in the wall on the left, with a narrow lane climbing alongside. Follow Queen Street, with its often ancient cottages, as far as you wish and then return to the start by taking the lane by the letterbox, which passes lovely old Forge Cottage at the top of the slope.

Compton Abdale

Getting there:	Compton Abdale lies south of the A40, 3½ miles NW of Northleach.
Park:	Near the crossroads at the centre of the village. (OS Landranger sheet 163. GR 061166).
Introducing the village	Five switchback country roads meander over the wolds towards Compton Abdale. Two of these meet to the west of the village, leaving four to form a crossroads in a watery hollow, from which the village extends in all directions. Approached from north, east or south, Compton Abdale is seen as a small village, snugly remote, and hemmed in by what that doyen of Cotswold authors, H.J. Massingham, called "the monster semi-circle of high, bare, smooth, symmetrical downs towards whose dorsal plane the village pokes its way".
	Two features, especially, draw visitors to this out-of-the-way village. One is St Oswald's Church, perched high above the crossroads, its tower adorned by an incredible collection of heraldic beasts – some say bears, others wolves, yet others, dogs – and its crocodile head, carved from local stone and spouting water from a powerfully flowing spring into a gigantic trough.
Refreshments:	Puesdown Inn (on A40, 1 mile NE).

A peep into the past

Compton Abdale grew up along a prehistoric trading route, the White Way, sweeping south from its junction with another ancient road, the Salt Way, a short distance to the north. The Romans, always good judges of suitable sites, built a fine villa nearby and by Norman times there was a water mill here. Later, the village became the property of St Oswald's Priory at Gloucester, which is how the church received its dedication.

Incredible though it may sound, Compton Abdale is one of those privileged villages to have had its history researched and recorded in a book. In 1993, the late Mrs Katja Kosmala, a native of Silesia who lived for many years in the village, published 'Compton Abdale in the Cotswolds', a beautifully produced volume telling the story of this tiny place.

Walkabout

Compton Abdale's layout at a crossroads, with no back lanes and only one public footpath linking two of its approach roads, restricts a walkabout to four short ambles from its centre. All of these are pleasant

Compton Abdale: the path up to the church

enough, offering views for those venturing north or south and a delightful roadside stream for company if strolling west.

1. The road eastwards, signposted Northleach, is especially interesting. This walk passes the former water mill, recently converted into a private house, before reaching what was once the mill pond, now two narrow lakes formed by damming a tiny rivulet. These lakes are the home of families of moorhens, which weave undisturbed through a miniature watery forest of horsetail stems. The woodland opposite provides habitat for tits and warblers, while the stone walls along the way support a carpet of moss, lichens and stonecrop.

2. Back at the crossroads, known as the Square, the testing climb to the church richly repays the effort. Some graves by the path are well worth watching out for: one is a chest tomb with a weathered head

carved on the top and holes for playing Nine Men's Morris still visible. Nearby, the stone to John Wilson, who died in 1735, has the wording of the inscription muddled, as though the mason had his mind on other things.

But it is the array of heraldic beasts, with staves and the assorted grotesque gargoyles on the tower, that are the chief attraction. Binoculars would be useful to study their detail. Inside the church, notice the mutilated carving believed by some to represent St George slaying the dragon. Others claim it is a Roman gravestone. Opinions vary too, about the species of bird depicted on the lectern – eagle, parrot, or hybrid, perhaps? However, there is no mistaking the identity of the creatures woven into the altar cloth, the work of skilful fingers with every detail perfectly captured.

3. Finally, the crocodile. Mrs Kosmala's researches revealed that it was the work of a local mason, George Curtis, who died in 1887, aged 83. Apparently, the locals ridiculed the carving at the time and old George took offence and left the village to end his days in Durham.

Notgrove

Getting there:	Notgrove lies 1 mile south of the A436, 3 miles north of Northleach.
Park:	Car park opposite village hall and bus shelter (O.S. Landranger Sheet 163. GR 108202)
Introducing the village	One of the smallest and least spectacular of the villages included in this book, Notgrove is a quiet, half-hidden, scattered little place, set amid walled fields in which sheep have grazed for centuries.
To those for whom countryside enjoyment means a leisurely amble along empty lanes, with trees in plenty and glimpses of distant landscape rewarding the mounting of every gentle rise, Notgrove is a delight. It stands high on the wolds, but the men who built its low stone cottages in ages past knew a thing or two about siting them to avoid the sweeping upland winds and they huddle snugly in their hollows, sheltered from the brunt of the blast.
The massive old barns, by contrast, stand on higher ground, defying the elements. Weather-beaten, and like the field walls, matted with moss and encrusted with lichen, they were built to last. Notice the dove holes in the gable of the largest, a reminder that birds were kept, not for decorative purposes, but to provide a change of diet from salted meat in severe winters.
The principal buildings – church and manor house – stand together unobtrusively on the southern edge of the village, as though setting the tone for this modest little place. They have their stories to tell, however, as we shall see when we peep into Notgrove's past.
Refreshments:	Plough Inn, Aston Blank (Cold Aston), 1½ miles east.

A peep into the past

Notgrove's history began 4,000 or so years ago. A mile north west from the village, alongside the A436, is Notgrove Barrow, a Neolithic burial mound which, when excavated during the last century, yielded the remains of a local chieftain, together with those of several women and children, including a baby. Human sacrifices, perhaps? Alas, we'll never know. Anyway, these, and samples of animal bones and pottery, can be seen in Cheltenham Museum.

However, the history of the village as we know it begins with the Romans. It is said that the little Norman church, like the even tinier Saxon building it replaced, stands on the site of a Roman cemetery. We have to take this on trust but at least we can see a precious fragment of

Saxon handiwork. This is a weathered little crucifix, built into the outer wall and passed on the way to the entrance, a real gem.

Inside the church is another exquisite miniature, this time a Virgin and Child in faded glass said to be early 14th century. There are also several reminders of people who helped to shape Notgrove's past. They include effigies of priests, one of a lady, and large monuments to the Whittingtons, descendants of the celebrated Dick, who were lords of the manor during the 16th and 17th centuries.

From the church entrance, the manor house is revealed in all its glory. Though dating back to the 17th century, it has seen many changes since the time of the Whittingtons, due partly to a disastrous fire. Over the churchyard wall can be seen an interesting dovecote, together with associated farm buildings.

Notgrove

Walkabout

1. From the car park, walk to the left up the hill. At the top, the spire of the church comes into view, at the end of the manor drive.

2. Turn left and follow the narrow road between farm buildings. This swings to the right by a huge barn and dips to a sharp left hand bend.

3. To see the church and manor house, leave the road at the bend and turn right. Retrace steps to the road.

4. Continue the descent. At the foot, the road swings left by a cottage. Climb to the village green. The car park is a short way to the left but you may care to explore the northern fringe of the village by turning right before returning to your car.

Notice the drinking trough, fed by a spring, and the paved standing for animals. And can you see the artificial house martins' nests under the eaves of the house opposite the car park?

Sherborne

Getting there:	Sherborne lies one mile north of the A40 and 4 miles east of Northleach.
Park:	By kerb along village street, near the school and post office. (O.S. Landranger Sheet 163. GR 174145).
Introducing the village	Strung out along the valley of the Sherborne Brook, a tributary of the River Windrush, Sherborne grew up as the estate village of the Duttons, a wealthy family who resided here for over 400 years. Following the death of the last of the line, in the 1980s, the estate was bequeathed to the National Trust and although Sherborne House and its stable block have been converted into luxury flats, much of the 4,000 acre estate is now managed to facilitate public access and in the interests of nature conservation.
Refreshments:	Fox Inn, Barrington Bridge (2 miles SE). Choice of inns at Northleach.

A peep into the past

Until the dissolution of the monasteries, Sherborne was a small village surrounded by the sheepwalks of Winchcombe Abbey, with the abbot's summer palace the only building of note. By 1651, however, the original Sherborne House had been built and the Dutton family were well established as lords of the manor.

A good deal about the Duttons can be discovered from studying the memorials in the church. An early member of the family, John (1598-1657), known as 'Crump', is said to have been on good terms with Oliver Cromwell, who allowed him to stock his new park with deer from Wychwood Forest. He later built a spectacular grandstand, Lodge Park, two miles south west of Sherborne, as a viewing place from which to watch the coursing of deer by greyhounds.

According to 'Crump' Dutton's memorial in the church, he was "master of a large fortune and owner of a mind equall to it, noted for his great hospitallity farr and neer and his charitable relief of ye poor." However, his claim to fame in the village is based chiefly on his ghost, which is reputed to have been seen driving a coach and horses from Sherborne House along the lonely road to Lodge Park.

Doorway – No. 88, Sherborne village

Walkabout

Sherborne is an exceptionally long village, extending for over a mile in a series of winding undulations, its east and west ends separated by Sherborne Park. There being no side streets and only one short back lane, the walkabout entails retracing steps, although with so much to see, this seems in no way repetitive.

1. With the post office on the right, walk along the pavement towards the west end of the village. Beyond the nursery on the left, in which a barn stands on elegant stone pillars, a high wall screens the great house. However, this can be glimpsed from the churchyard, which is reached along a signposted path from the road.

2. St Mary Magdalene Church dates from the 14th century but the greater part of the present building is 17th century or later. The lofty interior is virtually a mausoleum to the Duttons, whose sumptuous monuments, and especially those by the eminent 18th century sculptors Rysbrack and Westmacott, dominate the chancel. By contrast, the plaque on the wall of the nave commemorating the birth in 1693 of Sherborne's most illustrious son, James Bradley, the third Astronomer Royal, is a modest affair.

3. Continue along the descending pavement. From the hollow there is a sweeping view of the long ornamental lake, complete with weir, that was created from the Sherborne Brook by the removal of thousands of tons of gravel, used in the construction of Avonmouth Docks, near Bristol. Water birds, especially mute swans, Canada geese and herons, can be viewed at leisure from this vantage point.

4. Continue, if so desired, as far as a crossroads, around which are grouped rows of 17th century cottages in long gardens. Retrace to the start. (A pleasant diversion can be taken by turning down the no-through-road on the left and following a footpath to the right and so back to the road via a hand-gate).

5. From the parking point, follow the pavement into the east end of the village. Here, the rows of cottages were rebuilt in about 1820 to create a model village of the kind then in fashion.

6. At the T-junction, turn right and follow the road as it climbs to a left hand bend. Here, opposite a side road, stands a cottage numbered 88, which incorporates a 12th century doorway with a carved tympanum, and which must either have once been a church or have been built from stone brought from the site of a demolished Norman church.

/ Northleach Area

Withington

Getting there:	Withington lies south of the A40 and A436, 5 miles west of Northleach.
Park:	As near as possible to the church (OS Landranger sheet 163. GR 032156).
Introducing the village	Withington is a large irregular village in the upper Coln valley. Its older part is grouped along a tangle of narrow high-banked roads near the church. Between 1891 and 1962 the village was bisected by the Andoversford Junction – Cirencester railway line and plenty of evidence of this – embankments and blue brick walls – survives today. There are some impressive buildings, including a lofty church, a fine old manor house, a former palace of the Bishops of Worcester, and a deceptively recent pub. The infant River Coln and a large lake add greatly to the beauty of the place.
Refreshments:	Mill Inn. Kings Arms Inn.

A peep into the past

A sizeable remnant of Withington's early history, in the form of a mosaic excavated from a Roman villa, can be seen in the British Museum. Today, the Norman church doorway is the oldest visible feature, but there is some good Cotswold stone building dating back to the 17th century, as will be revealed on the walkabout.

By 1820, when the author of 'Rural Rides', William Cobbett, came on horseback through Withington, the village's fortunes were at a low ebb. "It was, and not so very long ago", he wrote, "a gay and happy place; but it now presents a picture of dilapidation and shabbiness scarcely to be equalled." The solitary exception was the church, which he thought "prettily situated" and likened it to a small cathedral.

Walkabout

This includes some footpath walking, which may be muddy after rain.

1. From the junction by the church, follow the Chedworth sign. Just beyond the school, a glimpse can be had of the finely proportioned 16th century manor house. The old petrol pumps a little further on have become relics of the past in the space of a few decades, as, in their time, did the village smithies that they replaced. Turn left at the

Withington crossroads

junction and then left again, passing Halewell, once the great house belonging to the Bishops of Worcester, on the right.

2. At the T-junction, turn right and walk down to the River Coln, beside which the Mill Inn stands in its extensive garden. The Mill may have the look of centuries but amazingly it was rebuilt as late as 1960, but with weathered stone from Northleach Prison.

3. Follow the 'Public path' sign on the right below the inn. The path follows the Coln and then the bank of a lake, on which moorhens, coots, dabchicks, mallard and occasionally swans can be seen. The route crosses two stiles before reaching a house and a minor road. Turn left here and pass the remains of a railway bridge. Keep on as far as a T-junction. The King's Arms Inn is on the right, up a lane signposted to the Roman villa and Yanworth.

4. To return to the Mill and the start, turn left along the winding road between high wooded banks. (No pavement – beware traffic).

5. St Michael's Church is well worth visiting. On the right of the main doorway is a fine cylindrical 'tea caddy' tomb, complete with ornate scroll supports and a neatly moulded 'lid'. Beyond the chevroned Norman doorway is an impressive spacious interior rich in memorials. Outstanding among these is that of the Howe family of Compton Cassey, dated 1651. The parents appear to be sitting in a box at the theatre, with their eight children, all kneeling and mourning and their short lives meticulously recorded below.

Equally poignant is the tombstone – brought inside to preserve it from the elements – of 'Jhon' Stockwell, who died of the plague and was buried here on 25th September 1665, the year of London's notorious outbreak. Was he a fugitive from that scourge, one wonders, and if so, was he the sole victim in this remote Cotswold village?

Burford Area

The middle reaches of the Windrush valley form the principal feature of this area. The River Windrush, supplemented by the waters of its tributary, the Sherborne Brook, writhes its way eastwards towards the Thames, its banks lined with as fair a selection of villages as can be found in any comparable part of the country.

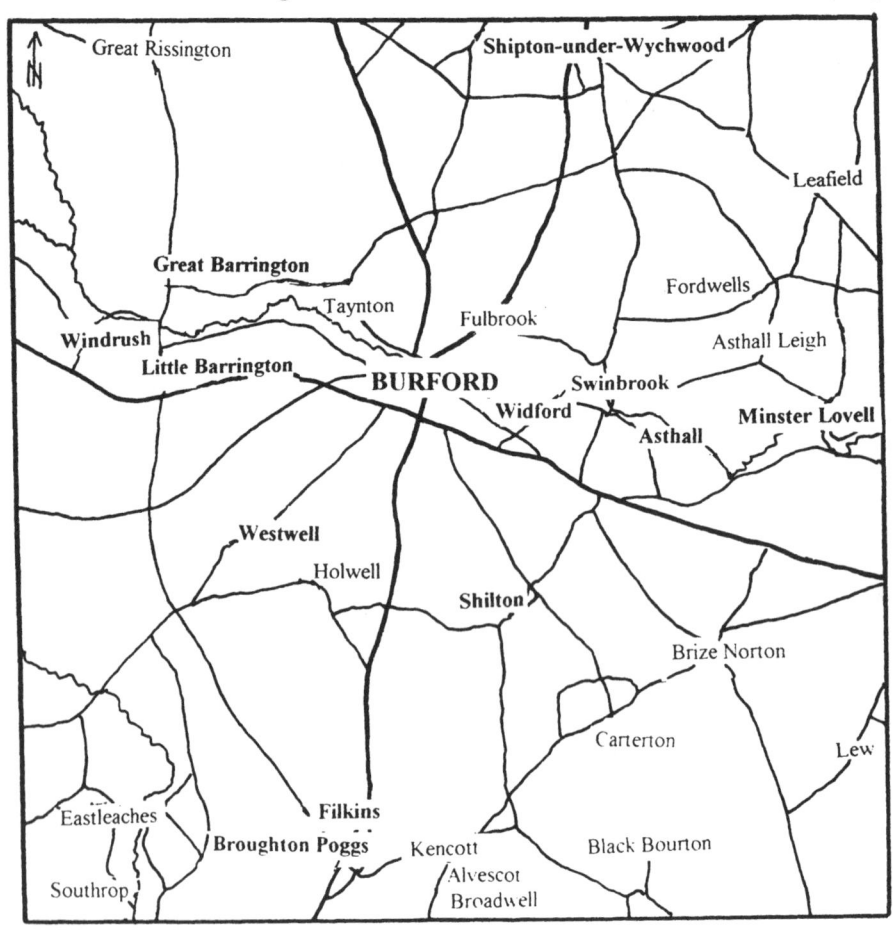

These villages – Windrush, The Barringtons, Taynton, Swinbrook, Asthall and Minster Lovell, together with Burford itself – were fashioned over the centuries from locally quarried limestone. This limestone, in particular that obtained from Taynton and the Barringtons, was considered the finest building stone available and was used for the rebuilding of St Paul's Cathedral and in the construction of, among other notable buildings, Windsor Castle, Blenheim Palace and many of the Oxford colleges.

The most famous of these quarries have long since been abandoned but the names of the master masons who worked them, such as Christopher Kempster of Burford and the Strong family of Taynton and Barrington, have their place in history. Happily, the 20th century produced its own outstanding craftsman in stone, George Swinford of Filkins, whose autobiography, 'Jubilee Boy', published shortly before his death, aged 100, in 1987, brings the story of the Burford area stone up to date.

The area's history is not confined to stone, however. Vestiges of Roman Akeman Street can be traced at Holwell and Asthall, while the romantic ruins of Minster Lovell's 15th century manor house, with its historic church and farm alongside, provide a fascinating glimpse into a way of life long since gone.

There are rich literary associations in the area. Compton Mackenzie wrote his novel 'Guy and Pauline' at Burford. The Mitford sisters, three of whom are buried at Swinbrook, wrote of girlhood both there and at Asthall, while 'The Countryman' magazine was for many years edited at Burford.

Burford

Aptly called 'The Gateway to the Cotswolds', this ancient Oxfordshire town, with its High Street climbing steeply from a handsome bridge over the Windrush, is generally acknowledged as one of the finest small towns in England.

Burford's prosperity was based on wool and stone. It was also renowned for brewing, bellfounding and saddle and bridle making – highly appropriate considering its importance as a staging post in the coaching era. The railway bypassed it however and the town we admire today, with superb church, Tolsey, and a wealth of outstanding buildings in stone and timber, was left virtually unscathed by the march of industrial progress.

Asthall

Getting there:	Asthall lies 1 mile north of the A40, 2.5 miles east of Burford.
Park:	Near the church. (O.S. Landranger Sheet 163. GR 288113)
Introducing the village	This tiny Oxfordshire village lies in the water meadows of the Windrush Valley, sufficiently below the relentlessly busy A40 to preserve its rural atmosphere. Grouped in casual fashion around a not-quite-square meadow, Asthall possesses almost all the features associated with the traditional English village – church, manor house, inn and attractive cottages set in pretty gardens. The school has long been converted into a private house but there is no mistaking its former identity. The Windrush, spanned by a picturesque bridge, loops round the village and delightful riverside walks can be taken upstream to Swinbrook or downstream to Worsham and Minster Lovell.
Refreshments:	The Maytime Inn.

A peep into the past

Asthall's oldest surviving man-made feature stands well to the south of the village and is passed, largely unnoticed, by countless people daily. This is the large tree-covered Saxon burial mound known as Asthall Barrow, dating from the 7th century AD, which commands the busy roundabout at the western end of the Witney bypass at the junction of the A40 and the B4047. Objects excavated from this cremation burial can be seen in the Ashmolean Museum at Oxford.

Traces of the Romans, though numerous, are harder to find. The line of their Akeman Street is shown on maps as passing close by on its journey from St Albans to meet the Fosse Way at Cirencester and the Windrush must have been crossed by a ford to the north-east of the village. Archaeological evidence of Roman buildings close by and further downstream near Worsham Mill has been unearthed in recent years but there is nothing to be seen today.

The church, dedicated to St Nicholas, dates from the Norman period but numerous additions and modifications were made prior to a heavy Victorian restoration in 1885. From the churchyard, a good view can be had of the manor house, an elegant building with gables and mullioned windows, built in traditional Cotswold style by Sir William Jones early in the 17th century.

Between 1920 and 1926, Asthall Manor was the home of David

Asthall Manor House and church

Freeman-Mitford, the second Lord Redesdale, and his wife Sydney, together with their son and six daughters. Two of these girls, Nancy and Jessica, were to write in later years of their childhood days at Asthall, giving what some regard as a distorted view of their life at that time.

What is certain is that all of the Mitford children, as part of their education, were given smallholdings and were encouraged to farm them economically. Their pocket money was earned from their raising of chickens, pigs and calves and they were expected to pay rent for their holdings in the same way as the estate tenant farmers.

The graves of three of the 'Mitford Girls', Nancy, Unity and Pamela, can be seen in Swinbrook churchyard.

Walkabout

1. The starting place for the walkabout, the churchyard, provides not only a memorable close up of the manor house but is notable for its collection of interesting tombstones. Perhaps the most striking of these is the Baroque bale tomb, complete with finial, of Harman Fletcher, a member of a wealthy Asthall family, who died in 1729.

This stands on the right of the path leading to the church porch and sadly is now in a somewhat dilapidated condition.

The church has a fine Norman arcade and a decorated 12th century tub font. However, the most impressive feature is the 14th century stone effigy of a lady in flowing robes, believed to be that of Lady Joan Cornwall, delicately carved and sheltered by a vast canopy. Above is some rare stained glass dating from the same period.

2. Follow the lane as it climbs to the left from the churchyard gate. Turn left at the junction and continue along the beech avenue to the next junction. It is at this point, where a footpath emerges from the right, that the line of Akeman Street passes closest to the village.

3. Turn left back into the village. There are several attractive cottages between the inn and the church.

4. For an unforgettable view of the church and manor house from the water meadows, take the right fork by the inn to reach a stile on the left just beyond the bridge. This gives access to the footpath to Swinbrook.

Filkins and Broughton Poggs

Getting there:	Filkins and Broughton Poggs lie off the A361, 5 miles south of Burford.
Park:	Filkins. Near the church. (O.S. Landranger Sheet 163. GR 238042).
Introducing the villages	Filkins and its tiny neighbour, Broughton Poggs, lie in the gentle south Cotswold countryside of south west Oxfordshire and are now happily bypassed by the bustling A361 linking Burford with Lechlade. Stone-built from local quarries, Filkins's rich history has been well recorded in a book, 'Jubilee Boy' (Filkins Press, 1987), essentially the life story of a local craftsman and centenarian, George Swinford, who lived his entire life in Filkins and established a small museum which is still open to visitors on Sunday afternoons during the summer months. A further attraction is the Cotswold Woollen Weavers, with its working weaving mill, exhibition gallery and shop, based in a fine 18th century barn in the centre of Filkins Village.
Refreshments:	Lamb Inn. Five Alls Inn.

A peep into the past

It is to the geological, rather than the historical past that the visitor to Filkins is inevitably drawn. For the limestone that has yielded the roofs, walls and fences that abound throughout the village came into being countless millions, rather than mere hundreds of years ago.

No one knows when Fikins's first quarries were dug. However, thanks to George Swinford, we do know that the stone they contained varied considerably, some being of Forest marble, whereas some was rich in fossils, ranging from ammonites to the remains of sharks.

In 1929, when he reopened Long Ground Quarry on the instructions of Sir Stafford Cripps, George Swinford discovered a French clay pipe that had belonged to a prisoner captured during the battle of Waterloo.

Between them, Cripps's money and Swinford's expertise ensured that Filkins remains a testimony to the quality of Cotswold stone. In the twenty or so years following the reopening of Long Ground Quarry, Swinford and his men extracted 91,000 slates, 11,000 cubic yards of building stone and 160 tons of paving stone, with which new buildings, including council houses, were constructed and older properties carefully repaired.

One writer once asked Swinford what was the secret in building the drystone walls which feature so prominently in the Filkins locality. "You've got to be really interested in the job and have a good eye," came

Stone slab fencing at Filkins

the reply. "There's always a stone for every place and a place for every stone."

Fortunately, this master craftsman managed to find time to write his autobiography, which is both a history of his village and an invaluable social document.

Walkabout

1. From St Peter's Church, built in the French Gothic style in the 1850s, walk into Filkins, passing the war memorial, with the Lamb Inn commanding the road junction. Continue straight on. The Swinford Museum, together with the tiny, cell-like lock-up, is soon reached on the left. Local legend has it that the wives of those imprisoned administered teapots of ale to their loved ones by poking the spout through the grill!

2. Some good traditional Cotswold stone cottages line both the main street and the tempting side street and lanes. The versatility of the stone – and of the men that fashioned it – is further revealed in the slab fences, known locally as planks, fronting the cottage gardens, and in the great barn now housing the Cotswold Woollen Weavers. Opposite the latter stands Filkins Hall, an early 20th century rebuilding of a Tudor house destroyed by fire in 1876. The stable block, with its belfry, predates the present house by about a century. This was the home of Sir Stafford Cripps, Chancellor of the Exchequer in the 1945 Labour government and a generous benefactor to the village.

3. To visit Broughton Poggs, retrace steps as far as Filkins Church and then continue to pass the village hall and the Five Alls Inn. Cross a road junction and the bridge over the Broadwell Brook (noting the former mill). Broughton Poggs church is reached via a public footpath along the drive to the hall (not the farm road). At a fork, turn left. The church, with its distinctive saddleback tower, is almost hidden from view by the adjacent farm buildings. Like Filkins church, it is dedicated to St Peter but is much older, being of early Norman origin with additions dating from the early 13th century to the Victorian era.

Great Barrington

Getting there:	Great Barrington lies 1 mile north of the A40, 3 miles west of Burford.
Park:	Near the war memorial and road junction at the western end of the main street. (O.S. Landranger Sheet 163. GR 208138).
Introducing the village	It would be hard to imagine a greater contrast between neighbouring villages than that distinguishing Great from Little Barrington. For whereas Little Barrington nestles intimately around its sloping green, on the south bank of the River Windrush, Great Barrington's single level street reaches out eastwards from a vast deer park some distance from the north bank. And although an extensive restoration scheme has largely made good the appalling dereliction that blighted it during the 1960s and 70s, Great Barrington remains a somewhat austere village by Cotswold standards, despite its eventful history and generous share of interesting buildings.
Refreshments:	The Fox Inn, Barrington Bridge (half a mile SW).

A peep into the past

Great Barrington lies at the heart of the stone-quarrying belt for which the Cotswolds are famous. This stone, somewhat confusingly known as inferior oolite, not because of its quality but for its position in the limestone strata, gave rise to the village we see today and to the 18th century mansion, Barrington Park, glimpsed only fleetingly on its terrace above the diverted River Windrush.

Originally the seat of the Brays, Barrington Park passed to Earl Talbot, Lord Chancellor in the reign of George II. He rebuilt it in 1738 and landscaped its grounds in the fashion of the time. Most of Great Barrington itself dates from this period, having been built as an estate village, and as such it remains to this day.

This accounts for its decline in the 1960s and 70s, when its owner, determined to resist what he saw as the take-over by outsiders of so many Cotswold villages, preferred instead to allow surplus housing to fall into ruin, a situation that has only been reversed since the 1980s.

Walkabout

The short stretch of field path walking between the church and the back lane can be avoided by retracing from the church to the war memorial and then turning to the right down the lane opposite.

Great Barrington church

1. From the war memorial, follow the pavement alongside the road signposted Little Barrington. Immediately beyond the entrance to the drive to Barrington Park, from which a glimpse can be had of the mansion itself, is the path leading to St Mary's Church. The churchyard is overlooked by the handsome 18th century stable block belonging to the great house. Notice the long stone bench by the churchyard wall, possibly removed from inside the church at the time of its drastic restoration in 1880.

2. St Mary's, though Norman in origin, retains little from that period apart from its vast decorated chancel arch. Its main features of interest are its monuments, which include the somewhat battered effigy of Captain Edmund Bray, who died in 1620 and is depicted wearing his sword on his right side. According to the 17th century county historian Sir Robert Atkyns, "the captain having unhappily killed a man, and been pardoned by Queen Elizabeth, in token of his contrition refused ever after to use his right hand."

By contrast, another Bray monument of a century later and erected to the memory of two young children who died of smallpox, depicts them journeying to heaven under the guidance of an angel.

3. On leaving the churchyard, cross the road to pass between stone pillars and through a gate on the left. Cross a small field to another gate and pass a burial ground on the right to reach a crossway via two kissing gates.

4. Keep straight on along the lane ahead, which runs roughly parallel to the main street. This lane offers pleasing views – of Little Barrington to the south and of the Windrush Valley eastwards, with the tip of Burford church spire visible in the distance.

5. Follow the lane to its junction with the eastern extremity of the main street, passing the former school on the left and the splendid village hall of 1935 on the right. Notice the skilfully converted barn, once a hollow ruin, at the lane end.

6. Walk back into the village. Many of the houses and cottages passed were derelict until the 1980s. The forge on the left has been worked by three generations of smiths and still thrives.

Those wishing to catch a glimpse of the deer in the park should follow the Great Rissington road for a short way, as far as wrought iron gates on the left. In the distance can be seen a domed 18th century dovecote, built to resemble a classical temple and complete with portico.

… *Burford Area*

Little Barrington

Getting there:	Little Barrington lies half a mile north of the A40, 3 mile west of Burford.
Park:	As near as possible to the top of the green. (O.S. Landranger Sheet 163. GR 207128)
Introducing the village	A village of picturesque cottages grouped round a green typifies for many the essence of rural England. In the case of Little Barrington however, the green is no ordinary expanse of well-tended grassland. Instead, the sloping hollowed-out green, complete with stream, is in fact the bed of a long since worked-out quarry, one of several for which this area of the Cotswolds was for long famous. Despite its close proximity to the A40, Little Barrington retains its air of quiet seclusion, with tempting lanes and footpaths leading off along the valley of the River Windrush, here on the last mile of its journey as a Gloucestershire river before becoming an Oxfordshire one.
Refreshments:	Fox Inn, Barrington Bridge (quarter of a mile NW). Inn for All Seasons (half a mile south on A40).

A peep into the past

The story of Little Barrington is bound up with that of the Strongs, a family of quarrymen and stonemasons. Timothy Strong, a Wiltshire man, moved to Little Barrington towards the end of the 16th century and with his son Valentine, began to work the quarries to the south of the village that were to produce stone for use in some of the country's finest buildings.

Appropriately, the Strongs went from strength to strength. Thomas, the third generation, was employed by Christopher Wren on the rebuilding of St Paul's Cathedral and St Stephen's, Walbrook after the great fire of London and it was he who laid the first stone of the new St Paul's in 1675.

Transporting Barrington stone to London was a colossal enterprise. Thomas Strong achieved it by constructing a wharf on the Windrush near the present Fox Inn and was thus able to send stone to Newbridge and thence down to the capital along the Thames.

After Thomas's death, his brother Edward with his son, also Edward, continued and expanded the family business, completing the rebuilding of St Paul's and embarking on numerous other prestigious works, including the Royal Hospital, Greenwich, Blenheim Palace, and several prominent buildings in Oxford and the Cotswolds.

Old cottages at Little Barrington

Walkabout

1. From the top of the green, walk along the lane on the left and on reaching the pump, turn right to pass the cottages on the west side of the green. These cottages, of which no two are alike, are chiefly 17th and 18th century and possess an irresistible appeal. Notice in particular the former smithy, with its distinctive windows and doorway, and the post office, with its wide porch.

2. At the foot of the green, cross the road and walk back up the slope to reach a minor road on the left by the phone box. This leads to St Peter's Church.

3. Before entering the churchyard, notice the two unusual vertical stones on the grass verge. These marked the limit of the churchyard before the surrounding wall was built. At that time the present road had not been constructed and access to the churchyard was from the riverside path walked later.

4. There are some good examples of early 18th century table tombs in the churchyard. Before entering the church, notice the fine sanctus bellcote and the tympanum over the north doorway. There is also a striking monument on the outside of the porch. This is in memory of the Tayler family and was erected by William Mury, a carpenter, who married into the family, in 1734.

5. St Peter's Church, though of Norman origin, retains only a south doorway and nave arcade from that period. Nevertheless, it is well worth seeing, especially for those interested in tracing the evolution of church architecture over the centuries.

6. On leaving the churchyard, continue the short distance along the road to reach a lane on the left, just before the spacious grounds of Barrington Grove, a fine late 18th century mansion, a glimpse of which can be had as the lane descends. At its foot, those wishing to see Barrington Mill (now a private house) should cross the footbridge for the quarter of a mile each way walk. Otherwise, continue along the riverside path, from which the church was reached before the building of the top road.

7. Back at the foot of the green, notice the sundial on the cottage on the right and the reset arched stone doorway, possibly 14th century, on the restored cottage on the left.

Minster Lovell (Old Minster)

Getting there:	Minster Lovell lies off the B4047, 4 miles east of Burford.
Park:	Follow Old Minster sign from B4047 to reach Wash Meadow car park on right, immediately beyond bridge. (O.S. Landranger Sheet 164. GR 318112).
Introducing the village	Minster Lovell is in reality two villages, separated by the B4047, formerly the A40. The modern village, together with Charterville Allotments, a settlement of bungalows in large gardens – built by Fergus O'Connor for the Chartist Land Settlement Project in 1847 – lies to the south of this road, while the original village, signposted Old Minster, is situated to the north, both of the B4047 and of the River Windrush. Old Minster is widely regarded as one of the most alluring villages in Oxfordshire. Beginning with its 15th century bridge spanning the Windrush, its attractions include cricket on the spacious riverside Wash Meadow, the timber framed Old Swan Hotel, and a street lined with lovingly maintained Cotswold stone cottages set in colourful gardens. This leads to one of the most appealing clusters of buildings in the entire Cotswolds, comprising historic church, hall ruins, and well preserved farm buildings featuring barns, a dovecote and a remnant of a priory chapel.
Refreshments:	Old Swan Hotel. White Lion Inn and New Inn (both on B4047).

A peep into the past

As can be seen from the beautifully produced historical guide to the village on sale in the church, Minster Lovell is an ancient place with a long and colourful history. In Norman times, when the manor belonged to the abbey of Ivry, it was enclosed by Wychwood Forest, but by 1441, when Henry VI gave the church and lands to his newly-founded Eton College, the village as we see it was taking shape and a few years later, William Lovell set about building a hall and church on the banks of the Windrush.

Legend has it that later in the 15th century, William's descendant, Francis, known as Lovell the Dog, on account of the family emblem, perished while hiding from Henry VII after the Battle of Stoke and his skeleton was not discovered until workmen came upon it by accident – seated at a table with pen and paper – over two hundred years later!

Minster Lovell – Church and Manor ruins

Walkabout

The field path linking the church with the car park may be muddy after rain.

1. From the car park, walk into the village. On the left, the site of a succession of watermills is now occupied by a conference centre. Turn right by the Old Swan Hotel. This ancient hostelry, with its steeply pitched roof of Stonesfield slates, retains its timber frame and may well date from the 15th century.

2. Continue along the gently climbing street. Its beauty is enhanced by the stream, a tributary of the Windrush, that flows along the left hand side, and is spanned by stone slab bridges. Some of the houses are thatched and several are centuries old. In some cases, their names indicate their former use, as with the Old Bakehouse (notice the bread oven projecting from the end wall) and the Old Post House.

3. Climb as far as the lane on the right leading down to the church and hall. St Kenelm's Church was so named after the 8th century boy king, son of Kenulf, King of Mercia, said to have been murdered in the Clent Hills and later buried alongside his father in Winchcombe Abbey. It was built in the 15th century, possibly by William Lovell, to a cruciform plan and stands on the foundations of an earlier church. Its light and spacious interior contains much of interest, including an alabaster tomb chest reputed to be that of Lovell himself, and some original stained glass.

4. Minster Lovell Hall, a classic romantic ruin, was once one of the grandest houses in Oxfordshire. It was built about 1432, by William, the seventh Lord Lovell, incorporating part of an earlier building and served as the manor house for more than three centuries until its dismantling by its then owner, the Earl of Leicester, in 1747. It was not until the 1930s that the ruins were restored by the Ministry of Works. Now under the care of English Heritage, the hall retains sufficient of its original layout to make a careful inspection well worth while.

5. Close by, and also under English Heritage care, are the barns and circular dovecote of Manor Farm, together with the scant remains of the 12th century chapel of St Cecilia – an archway embedded in the farmhouse wall overlooking the churchyard.

6. To make the walkabout into a circular stroll, go through the stile near the bottom right hand corner of the churchyard and follow the clear field path over two more stiles, back to the Wash Meadow car park.

Shilton

Getting there:	Shilton can be approached either from the A361 or the B4020. It lies 3 miles SE of Burford.
Park:	Near to the ford in the centre of the village (O.S. Landranger Sheet 163. GR 268086).
Introducing the village	Shilton is one of the best kept secrets in the south Cotswolds. It lies away from busy roads in the shelter of the valley of the Shill Brook. A contributory cause of its obscurity may well be its close proximity to Carterton, the sprawling 'garrison town' associated with the RAF base at Brize Norton. Despite this, Shilton cannot fail to delight anyone seeking picture-postcard perfection. It possesses all the essential ingredients – a stream with a ford, a pond with attendant ducks, well cared-for cottages in colourful gardens, an ancient church and a friendly inn.
Refreshments:	Rose and Crown Inn.

A peep into the past

Out on a limb in the Oxfordshire Cotswolds, Shilton's history has always been one of comparative isolation. On early 19th century maps it is shown as being part of Berkshire, one of many tiny 'islands' that once existed in the heart of other counties, in this case Oxfordshire.

At the time of the dissolution of the monasteries by Henry VIII in 1538, the manor of Shilton belonged to the Cistercian monks of Beaulieu Abbey, Hampshire.

Until the early years of the 20th century, the countryside around Shilton still retained its centuries-old pastoral character. However, in 1901, a William Carter bought some land from the Duke of Marlborough a mile to the south east of Shilton to establish a colony of smallholders and market gardeners. Given the name Carterton, the settlement grew rapidly during the 1930s with the coming of the Brize Norton RAF base and is now a prosperous town.

Despite Carterton's alien presence nearby, and the constant whine of jet engines above, Shilton retains its country village atmosphere without acquiring the self-conscious air of certain better known Cotswold beauty spots. It owes a great deal of its charm to the Shill Brook, a Thames tributary flowing through the village from its source at the hamlet of Signet, a couple of miles distant. A well trodden footpath follows the west bank of this delightful stream from Shilton churchyard southwards

Shilton ford

for over two miles to Alvescot, another village uncomfortably close to Carterton.

Although Shilton cannot lay claim to having witnessed any great national event, it achieved fame for a brief period during the mid 17th century through a remarkable schoolmaster. The then rector of Bampton, the Rev. Samuel Birch, having been driven from his living for political reasons, established a school at Shilton and is reputed to have run it so successfully that fourteen of his pupils later became members of Parliament. One of these was Robert Harley, Earl of Oxford, a distinguished statesman during the reign of Queen Anne.

Walkabout

1. From the ford, walk along Church Lane, which climbs eventually to reach the Church of the Holy Rood. Away to the east over the Shill

Brook can be seen a round medieval dovecote standing in the grounds of Manor Farm. There is a thriving rookery nearby.

2. The church stands at the southern extremity of the village. It is Norman in origin and still retains its nave and south aisle from that period. There are several pleasing later features, the most striking of which is the square 14th century font, on the sides of which are depicted in crude workmanship scenes from the crucifixion. There are also traces of early wall paintings.

3. Follow the narrow road as it winds by the old school and between stone walls to pass attractive cottages in well-tended gardens.

4. On reaching the main street, turn right. Almost opposite stands Shilton House, with its 1678 datestone in the central gable. This is a finely proportioned Cotswold stone house with characteristic mullioned and transomed windows and ball finials surmounting its gables.

5. Back at the start, cross the footbridge to get a closer view of the dovecote.

6. Finally, the road passing the inn can be followed as far as the bridge spanning the Shill Brook. More interesting cottages and colourful gardens are passed on the way.

Shipton-under-Wychwood

Getting there:	Shipton-under-Wychwood lies on the A361, 4 miles NE of Burford.
Park:	On lane by green leading to church. (O.S. Landranger Sheet 163. GR 279179).
Introducing the village	Three west Oxfordshire villages – Shipton, Milton and Ascott – bear the name of Wychwood, the ancient royal hunting forest, a small part of which still survives a few miles to the east. Shipton-under-Wychwood is the largest and arguably the most attractive of the trio, despite its position straddling the A361, and the curious traveller will discover plenty of interest – a lofty church, elegant houses, a historic inn, a spacious green, fine trees and attractive gardens.
Refreshments:	Shaven Crown Inn. Red Horse Inn. Lamb Inn.

A peep into the past

Shipton-under-Wychwood has had a colourful history. The powerful Neville family held the manor in the 15th century and later, when ownership transferred to the Crown, a royal hunting lodge was established at Langley, two miles distant. Stone from the lodge is incorporated into the farm that now stands on the site.

One of Shipton's most illustrious rectors was John Foxe, who during his ministry (1563-1587) wrote his 'Book of Martyrs' here. Legend has it that the village was also the home of the father of William Langland, author of 'Piers Plowman'. The poet is said to have spent his boyhood here before embarking on a monastic life at Malvern.

Needless to say, Shipton's history has always been linked inextricably with that of Wychwood Forest. Many are the tales recorded concerning deer poaching and of the battles – of wits and of the physical kind – between poachers and gamekeepers. Getting the illicitly obtained venison to Oxford market without detection was a problem that Walker, the Shipton carrier, finally solved – by fitting a false bottom to his cart!

Walkabout

1. This begins at the top of the green. A memorial fountain stands here to the 17 Shipton parishioners who died in 1874 when the 'Cospatrick', the ship on which they were emigrating to New Zealand, was destroyed by fire off Tristan da Cunha.

2. Walk down to St Mary's Church. In the churchyard is one of the most unusual tombs in the Cotswolds. Dated 1734, it marks the grave of the Morgan family and is a variation of the bale top design but with three decks, all ornately decorated with cherubs, garlands and foliage.

Inside the church, which dates from about 1200, can be seen a 15th century font embellished with the bear-and-ragged staff emblem of the Earl of Warwick and some impressive monuments ranging in age from the 14th to the 18th century.

Behind the church is the distinctive Prebendal House, now a nursing home. Built by Christ Church, Oxford, possibly as early as the 16th century, it stands in spacious grounds leading down to the River Evenlode.

2. On leaving the churchyard, walk along the footpath to the right alongside. This passes the former village school, built in the gabled Gothic style by the architect G.E. Street, who restored the church, in the 1850s, and now tastefully converted into a private house.

3. On reaching the A361, turn left and left again to pass the Red Horse Inn. Continue along the main street. Opposite the green stands the Shaven Crown Inn, one of the most historic hostelries in the

"The Shaven Crown"

Cotswolds. It dates from the 15th century and as its name suggests, formerly had a monastic connection, having been built as a guest house for nearby Bruern Abbey. Every effort has been made to retain the inn's unique medieval features, which include a central hall, a four-centred archway, a paved courtyard and traditional Cotswold mullioned windows.

4. Continue to reach the stables, yew hedge and wrought iron gates of Shipton Court. This magnificent house is Jacobean, having been built by a prominent landowning family, the Lacys, in 1603. Opposite is a splendid lime avenue leading to what must surely be one of the loveliest cricket grounds in the country.

5. Those wishing to take a circular walkabout should continue as far as Plum Lane on the left. Follow this, noting the square gabled former dovecote on the left, as far as the next junction. Turn left here along Mawles Lane, with its green banks, and follow it back to the A361. Turn right here to regain the village green.

Swinbrook and Widford

Getting there:	Swinbrook and Widford lie 1½ miles north of the A40, 2 miles east of Burford.
Park:	Swinbrook. Close to the tiny green, opposite the church. (O.S. Landranger Sheet 163. GR 281122).
Introducing the villages	Like its neighbour, Asthall, Swinbrook is a small village by the River Windrush, differing only in being on the north bank. Less than half a mile to the west, and reached by footpath, is all that remains of the village of Widford, notably the little Church of St Oswald, standing alone in the fields. Small and unpretentious it may be but Swinbrook has a wealth of historic and literary associations. Add to these the compelling attraction exerted by a lost village and the result is a corner of the Oxfordshire Cotswolds of exceptional interest.
Refreshments:	The Swan Inn, Swinbrook.

A peep into the past

For five centuries, Swinbrook was the home of the Fettiplaces, wealthy landowners whose fine manor house disappeared without trace soon after the line died out in 1805. Their incredible monuments dominate the village church, in contrast to the modest gravestones in the churchyard of the famous 'Mitford Girls' – Nancy, Unity and Pamela – later residents of this attractive little place.

Unlike Swinbrook's manor house, that of Widford has survived, whereas the village itself has been long deserted and is now merely a few humps and hollows to the north and west of the church.

Romance and mystery, in other words, are strong attractions in this corner of Oxfordshire and for those who like an absorbing ghost story, Katherine Briggs's 'Hobberdy Dick', set in and around Widford Manor, provides additional interest to an already rewarding visit.

Walkabout

The field path to Widford can be muddy after rain.

1. From Swinbrook's tiny green, walk along the lane by the phone box. Go left when the lane forks and follow an enchanting little stream up

Swinbrook Green

to a ford. Cross by the footbridge and turn left along the road as far as the churchyard gate on the right.

2. Swinbrook churchyard has a superb collection of late 17th and early 18th century table tombs. The work of local masons, they are intricately adorned, with cherubs and floral designs prominent and with half-cylindrical tops. In contrast are the plain stones marking the graves of Nancy and Unity Mitford on the far side of the churchyard, the former bearing a representation of a mole. A third sister, Pamela, is buried some distance away.

3. The interior of St Mary's Church is full of interest. The clear glass in the huge east window of the chancel ensures that the rich array of contents can be clearly seen. They include two immense monuments to the Fettiplace family, each depicting three noblemen reclining on

stone shelves resembling primitive bunk beds. Both give a clear idea of the costume of the period.

Close by can be seen 15th century misericords (seats with carved undersides) while a window in the south aisle contains a collection of fragments of 15th century glass painstakingly salvaged following the explosion nearby of a German bomb in 1940.

Also of interest in the nave are the colourful monument affixed to a pillar of John Goddard, who died in 1623, and a well-preserved table of benefactions, detailing the charitable bequests made by wealthy individuals to the local poor.

4. Walk through the churchyard and leave by the hand-gate on the left. This leads to the footpath to Widford, which passes between walls before crossing a field to reach St Oswald's Church. Simple and plainly furnished, this little church nevertheless has a strong appeal, not least because its two most distinctive features, wall paintings and Roman pavement, were not discovered until it was restored from virtual ruin in 1904. Sadly, vandalism has necessitated the covering over of the pavement but the badly faded paintings – of St Christopher in the nave and of the Living and the Dead Kings in the chancel – still make considerable impact.

5. Continue the walk, if so desired, to the drive connecting Widford Manor with the Burford-Asthall road. Bird life on the large pond to the left can best be seen from the bridge over the Windrush.

6. Retrace to Swinbrook, keeping straight on at the churchyard gate to pass between cottages. The Fettiplaces' manor house stood away to the right, between the church and the river.

Westwell

Getting there:	Westwell lies 1 mile south of the A40 and 3 miles SW of Burford.
Park:	As near as possible to the village pond. (O.S. Landranger Sheet 163. GR 224100).
Introducing the village	Close to the Gloucestershire border, Westwell is aptly named, being the furthest west village in Oxfordshire. Small, somewhat remote, and lying in comparatively flat and unremarkable south Cotswold countryside, it is nevertheless a delightful village, with its mellow stone buildings grouped casually around a green. As one writer put it: "Surely nothing could be more pleasurable than to sit on the green by the duck-pond in spring sunshine surrounded by such a lovely sight."
Refreshments:	Choice of inns and teashops in Burford.

A peep into the past

Westwell is one of those fortunate villages about which a well-researched history has been written. This was the work of a former rector, the Rev. A.S.T. Fisher, who was also responsible for the excellent church guide, reproduced, like the book, in the rector's own neat hand.

From this guide, we learn that the village owes its name to the well, near the churchyard gate, which has the distinction of being the most western spring in Oxfordshire. The first settlement, all trace of which has long since disappeared, was a Bronze Age henge which was situated to the east of the present village. The top of a rough-hewn altar stone, discovered under the chancel floor in 1933 and replaced, is believed to have belonged to a Saxon chapel that served the village before the present Norman church was built.

From the Norman de Hastings family, Westwell passed to the Knights Hospitallers and then to the monks of Edington, Wiltshire. Following the dissolution of the monasteries, it became the property of Christ Church, Oxford, in whose ownership it remained until its sale to Sir Sothern Holland in 1912.

It is to a 19th century rector that we owe one of our most popular hymns. The Rev. J.E. Bode wrote several hymns for use in his church but it is for his 'O Jesus, I have promised to serve Thee till the end', written for his own children's confirmation, that he is best remembered.

Burford Area 129

Westwell pond, green and war memorial

Walkabout

This consists merely of a short stroll over the green and along the village street, with the option, for those wanting more exercise, of wandering along any of the four minor roads and two footpaths radiating from the village.

1. The green itself provides a great deal of interest. Apart from the pond, with its ducks and moorhens and the mossy stone conducting water from the spring to the pond, the unusual 1914-18 war memorial should on no account be missed. Made from roughly-hewn stone, it incorporates the brass figure '1' from the Cloth Hall at Ypres, destroyed in the conflict, and commemorates two brothers.

2. St Mary's Church stands overlooking the green, its churchyard containing an appealing array of tombstones, including good examples of bale top tombs marking the graves of prosperous 17th century woolmen. No less than 52 different species of lichens have been recorded on gravestones in this churchyard.

The unusual lead and tiled wooden bellcote dates from a drastic restoration carried out in 1869. Inside the church however, are many old and distinctive features, including a fine early 13th century font, a monument to Richard Thorneton, a 17th century rector, and a vast carved memorial depicting Charles Trinder, who died in 1657, seen kneeling before a cross with his wife and fourteen children.

The rose window at the east end of the church is a very rare feature. Further interest is provided by a small display of Roman and medieval pottery found in the vicinity.

3. Alongside the church is a handsome late 17th century rectory, while across the road, veiled by trees, can be glimpsed the manor house, part of which dates from Tudor times, and which is approached along a drive with gateposts topped by carved sphinxes.

4. The short stroll reveals attractive cottages, noble barns, including one a short way down the drive past the phone box with an exceptionally ornate finial, a circular dovecote, and a Victorian post-box, resplendent in its spruced-up state.

Windrush

Getting there:	Windrush lies half a mile north of the A40, 4 miles west of Burford.
Park:	As near as possible to the church. (O.S. Landranger Sheet 163. GR 193131).
Introducing the village	The village of Windrush takes its name from the river on which it stands and though small, its appearance is entirely in keeping with the image its lovely name suggests. A tiny triangular green, graced by an avenue of lime trees leading to the church, marks the village centre. Four roads radiate from here, two of which link Windrush with the A40, sweeping along the ridge barely half a mile distant. The River Windrush itself is hidden from view at this particular spot but its charms are revealed on the walkabout, as is much else of interest in this appealing little village.
Refreshments:	Fox Inn, Barrington Bridge (three quarters of a mile east). Inn for All Seasons (on A40, 1½ miles SE).

A peep into the past

It is hardly surprising that Windrush displays numerous examples of the skilful use of stone, for its quarries yielded some of the finest stone in the Cotswolds.

Most of this stone was obtained from adits and galleries similar to those of coal mines, the blocks being levered on to low trolleys and hauled to the surface by horses. In 1839, Windrush was visited by members of the Royal Commission appointed to select stone for the rebuilding of the Houses of Parliament and they were so impressed by the resistance to weathering of the churchyard monuments that they chose Windrush stone for the work.

These famous quarries had closed by 1900, chiefly because of labour problems aggravated by newly-imposed safety regulations.

Walkabout

This includes a short stretch of field-path walking between Windrush Mill and the village, with 3 stiles on the way (one abnormally high!). Be prepared for mud after rain.

1. Before entering the churchyard, there are several features worth seeing beneath and within the churchyard wall. To the right of the gate is an old pumphead, while alongside stands the mounting block that served horseriding churchgoers in years gone by. To the left of the gate, alongside the official war memorial, is a memorial stone to a young airman who, when flying his unarmed training plane from the nearby airfield one night during the Second World War, lost his life by ramming an enemy bomber which was attacking his base.

2. Enter the churchyard. On the right of the path is an exceptionally fine collection of tombs, chiefly 18th century, and consisting of a range of variations on the table type. One in particular, dating from 1713, has a roll top similar to an earlier wool-bale design, with a ram's head set in its scalloped end.

3. Framing the Norman south doorway of the church are two rows of striking stone beak-heads, perfect in their execution, each one subtly different from its neighbours. Considering their exposed state, they are remarkably well preserved.

4. Within, St Peter's is comparatively plain, having suffered a drastic restoration in 1874. Nevertheless, there is plenty to see, especially the outward-leaning jamb shafts of the chancel arch, the lifelike ram's head corbel on the arcade and a memorial stone dated 1597, on which the inscription, though clearly legible, lacks spacing.

5. From the green, walk along the Sherborne road. To the left stands a fine 18th century farmhouse with characteristic Cotswold features. Opposite, Pear Tree Cottage has an early pointed arch doorway, possibly Tudor and inserted later. Below, on the left, an early 20th century cottage has the datestone 'Richard Tomes, 1668' inserted into its wall.

6. Follow the road past the old school and several good looking houses, as far as the lane leading to the mill, on the right alongside a house, 'The Barn'. On reaching the 17th century former corn mill, aptly described by one author as "a romantic, rubbly, rustic stone building", follow the footpath to the left to see the river and then retrace to take the right hand path, which leaves the mill grounds over a stone stile. There are good views along the valley at this point.

7. Turn sharp right up the field bank to reach the high stile remarked on earlier. Cross another in 30 metres (stone this time) and continue between walls to reach a lane leading back up to the village street and the start. Any remaining time can be well spent wandering along any or all of the three other lanes leading out of the village.

Burford Area 133

Windrush church door – bird beak ornamentation

Fairford Area

This small area of the south Cotswolds, through which flow two of the region's loveliest rivers on the final stages of their journey to the Thames, boasts no hills or dramatic scenery. Instead, its appeal lies in the gentleness of its terrain, with its landscaped parkland, picture-postcard villages and stretches of water created in recent years by gravel extraction.

First and foremost, however, it is the character of the two rivers, the

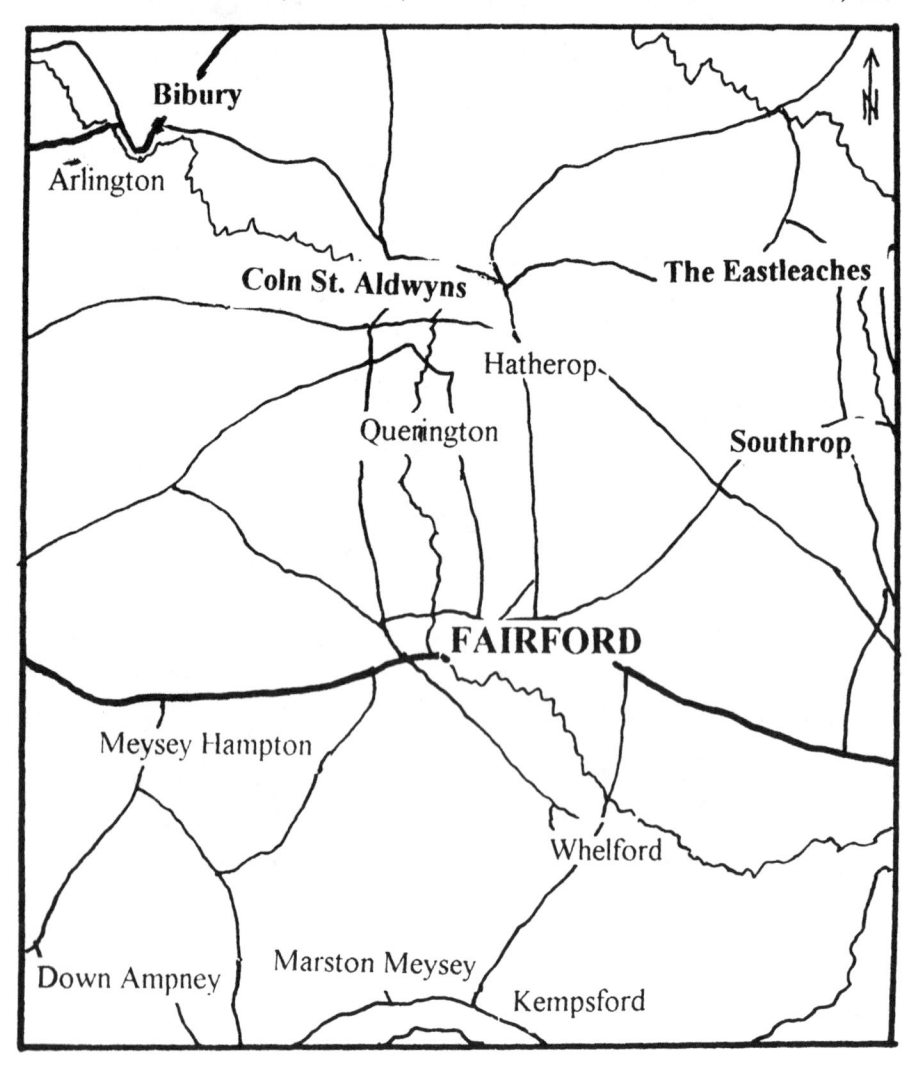

Coln and the Leach, that account for the spell that this area casts on those who take the trouble to get to know it intimately. This is particularly the case with the Coln-side village of Bibury which the poet and craftsman William Morris declared to be the loveliest village in England. Bibury, incidentally, gave rise to one of the earliest and best-loved of all books on the region, 'A Cotswold Village' by J. Arthur Gibbs, the Victorian squire of the nearby hamlet of Ablington.

A somewhat furtive stream compared with the Coln, the Leach is nevertheless an appealing little river and nowhere more so than where it flows beneath Keble's Bridge linking the charming Eastleaches, Turville and Martin. Downstream, and accessible by footpath, is Southrop, another delightful village of mellow stone with a tiny church whose prize possession is an exquisitely decorated font.

Fairford

A pleasant little market town, grouped around a square, with parkland forming its northern extremity, Fairford's fame rests primarily on the 15th century stained glass windows of its parish church. Made in the workshop of Barnard Flower, master glass painter to Henry VII, this glass is widely regarded as the finest collection to have survived the ravages of the Puritans. The church also contains much fine woodcarving, including misericords depicting everyday country scenes of five centuries ago.

Notable buildings overlooking the square include the early 18th century former free school, bearing plaques to esteemed teachers, and the rambling Bull Hotel, built in the 17th century and long famous as an anglers' hostelry.

Fairford possesses an extensive network of public footpaths, which enable walkers to follow the River Coln from the converted water mill on the edge of the town through the nearby complex of lakes formed by gravel digging. These provide the ideal habitat for a range of water birds, including mute swans, Canada geese, several species of ducks, coots and great-crested grebes.

Bibury

Getting there:	Bibury lies on the B4425, 6 miles NE of Cirencester.
Park:	By the riverside pavement on the B4425 near the bridge and Swan Hotel. (OS Landranger Sheet 163. GR 116069)
Introducing the village	This gem among villages needs little introduction for, since William Morris declared it to be the loveliest village in England in the 1870s, its treasures have lured generations of visitors. First and foremost among these treasures is the River Coln, here emerging from its secret upper stage to sweep boldly into the final phase of its journey to the Thames. The Coln is a famous trout stream and the farming of brown trout began here on a former watercress farm in 1902. Following the depletion of stock in the drought of the 1970s, these native fish were replaced by North American rainbow trout, although plenty of plump 'free range' browns can be spotted downstream. Arlington, up the hill from the bridge, merges with Bibury. Its two main attractions, the museum housed in a former watermill and its celebrated Row, are better known to visitors than the centre of Bibury itself, which lies off the B4425 in the direction of Burford, and which includes a superb church with the village school alongside and excellent examples of traditional Cotswold stone cottages.
Refreshments:	Swan Hotel. Catherine Wheel Inn, Arlington.

A peep into the past

Bibury originated as a Saxon settlement. St Mary's Church, though enlarged and modified over the centuries, contains much Saxon work, some of which, including a gravestone incorporated into the north wall, can be seen from the outside. The churchyard is full of interest, with an outstanding collection of table tombs marking the graves of prosperous 17th and 18th century woolstaplers and clothiers. The creeper-clad wall of Bibury Court, built by the landowning Sackvilles in 1633 and now an hotel, makes an impressive backdrop.

The interior of the church offers yet more memorable sights, including the Karl Parsons window of 1927, depicting the local coach, and which featured in the 1992 Royal Mail Christmas stamp.

A watermill was recorded at Arlington in the Domesday Book, although the present building dates from the 17th century. At various times it served as a corn mill but in its early years it was employed in fulling cloth produced by the weavers at nearby Arlington Row.

Arlington Row

This much photographed row may well have been a monastic barn before conversion into weavers' cottages. The low-lying ground between the row and the B4425, now a wildfowl reserve, is known as Rack Isle, on account of its use by the weavers as a drying ground for their cloth. Both the row and Rack Isle are in the care of the National Trust.

To the north of Bibury, and reached along an unclassified road from the bridge, is the attractive hamlet of Ablington, home of J. Arthur Gibbs, author of 'A Cotswold Village', a minor country classic written shortly before his early death in 1898. Gibbs's former home, the 16th century manor, can be glimpsed over its surrounding wall.

Walkabouts

Short walkabout

1. Follow the pavement with the river on the right. Pass 2 one-way streets on the right and climb to a path by a phone box leading to a road down to the church and school.

2. Leaving the churchyard, turn left and follow the road to the B4425. Cross the footbridge to reach Arlington Row. At the end of the row keep to the right over the footbridge and continue to reach the B4425 opposite the museum.

3. Turn right and cross the footbridge back to the start.

Longer walkabout

About one and a half miles and including field-path which may be muddy after rain.

1. Follow the pavement with the Coln on the right, as far as the one-way street leading to the church and school. From the churchyard gate, turn right and climb back to the B4425. Turn right and soon right again (Coln St Aldwyns sign).

2. In a few yards, turn right yet again down a lane to pass Bibury Court on the right. Cross the bridge and swing right, passing the old mill before climbing to the left to a gate.

3. Turn right here. Climb to another gate and follow the wall on the right to a stone stile at the edge of the beech woodland. Continue, to reach steps leading down to Arlington Row.

4. Go through the stile and turn left to pass in front of the row. At its end, cross the footbridge on the right and continue to reach the B4425 opposite the museum.

5. Turn right and cross the footbridge back to the start.

Coln St Aldwyns

Getting there:	Coln St Aldwyns lies midway between the B4425 and the A417, 2 miles SE of Bibury and 3 miles north of Fairford.
Park:	Along the lane leading to the church. (O.S. Landranger Sheet 163. GR 144053)
Introducing the village	A chain of delightful villages line the banks of the lovely River Coln after it passes beneath the Fosse Way at Fossebridge and wriggles its way towards Fairford. Bibury, by far the largest, naturally finds a place in this book; the problem has been which of the others, all of which clamour for inclusion, should be chosen. After much deliberation, Coln St Aldwyns gets this coveted place. It is grouped engagingly around a tiny green at a crossroads of minor routes, above a dramatic bend in the river from which it takes its name. Its church tower, with its distinctive turrets with their crocketed pinnacles, draws the eye and its cottages, cosy inn and two old watermills by the beguiling Coln, complete the picture.
Refreshments:	The New Inn.

A peep into the past

Coln St Aldwyns is reputed to have taken its name from Ealdwine, a hermit saint, although some sources attribute it to St Athelwine, bishop of Lindsey in the 7th century. It was first established as a settlement near the meeting place of Roman Akeman Street, linking Corinium (Cirencester) with Virulamium (St Albans) and the Salt Way, extending from Droitwich to Lechlade. Both ancient ways could be traced in their entirety in the area until the 18th century, when the power of the local landowners was such that Samuel Blackwell of nearby Williamstrip was able to close a three-mile length of Akeman Street to ensure his privacy! Park-making also obscured the original line of the Salt Way as it negotiated the Coln near the village, so that we need to project both routes on the OS map in order to establish their former positions.

Like the other Cotswold rivers, the Coln powered a number of watermills, the earliest of which were already in existence at the time of the Domesday Book in 1086. Two mills, standing no doubt on original sites, have survived to the present day at Coln St Aldwyns. Both are passed on the walkabout and the second, by the road to Quenington, was still grinding corn until the 1920s.

The Church of St John the Baptist, of which John Keble, author of 'The

Christian Year', served as curate to his father, dates from the Norman period, as can be seen from the impressive south doorway. It stands alongside a Tudor manor house, one of two fine houses in the vicinity, the other being the 17th century Williamstrip Park, a short distance away to the east.

Walkabout

The two short stretches of footpath may be muddy after rain.

1. Walk towards the church, noting the memorial cottages on the left, dating from 1947 and built from stone and timber resulting from the partial demolition of Williamstrip Park. By the church gate are the Wilkins charity almshouses, built in 1916. The churchyard entrance is flanked by two distinctive Victorian Gothic buildings, the vicarage and the former village school.

2. Before entering the church through the late Norman south doorway, with its fine chevron work and striking dragons' heads, do not miss two further impressive examples of early carving overhead – a man pursued by a demon, which is about to devour his hand, and a fierce cat-like creature with an evil toothy leer. The door itself is in fact a door within a door and must be centuries old. After all this, the interior, heavily restored in the 1850s, is a disappointment.

3. Back in the churchyard, it is worth looking over the north wall for a glimpse of the 16th century manor house, seat of the Hicks-Beach family, whose graves lie nearby.

4. From the churchyard gate, turn right along a pleasant lane, which eventually becomes a footpath and descends to cross the Coln by a footbridge. A fine old watermill, now a private house, can be seen on the right. Turn left along the drive to reach a road, either directly or along the river bank, reached through a field gate on the left, just beyond a house.

5. Turn left back into the village, passing the attractive old corn mill. The creeper-clad New Inn, with its interesting outbuildings, including one with doveholes, is on the right.

6. The tiny village green, dominated by its horse chestnut tree, marks the village centre. Here, opposite the post office/shop, a telephone is tucked neatly into a stone box, roofed, appropriately enough, with genuine Cotswold slates.

In Coln St Aldwyns

The Eastleaches

Getting there:	The Eastleaches lie 2 miles west of the A361 and 4 miles north of Lechlade.
Park:	Eastleach Turville. As near as possible to the Victoria Inn at the junction of the unclassified roads signposted to Fairford and Burford. (O.S. Landranger Sheet 163. GR 199052).
Introducing the village	The Eastleaches – Turville and Martin – face one another across the delightful little River Leach, their Norman churches merely a couple of stone-throws apart, their harmonious unity reinforcing the impression of a single village as suggested by the signposts pointing in their direction. Two bridges connect the villages, a road bridge and a long footbridge of large flat stones known as Keble's Bridge. This family, from whom the celebrated John, founder of the Oxford Movement and author of 'The Christian Year' was descended, were lords of the manor of Eastleach Turville in the 16th century. Turville is by far the larger of the two, its main street sweeping gracefully up from the river and lined with interesting Cotswold stone cottages. Martin, by contrast, is grouped close to its redundant church, which features as a backdrop on countless calendars and postcards of the daffodil-lined banks of the Leach in spring.
Refreshments:	The Victoria Inn, Eastleach Turville.

A peep into the past

The two Eastleaches once belonged to two different manors and this accounts for the close proximity of the churches. Both villages enjoyed prosperity during the boom years of sheep farming but following the enclosure of the open downs during the latter half of the 18th century, corn growing transformed the lower Leach Valley.

It is hard to realise today the extent of the hardship experienced by the farm labourers in this quiet valley as machinery made its impact on the land. By 1830, these desperate men were driven to "riotously and tumultously assembling together" and several hated threshing machines were destroyed. Punishment was severe and several Eastleach men were either transported or sentenced to hard labour at Northleach Prison.

In 1867, the Eastleaches became the property of Sir Thomas Bazley of Hatherop and many of the later buildings date from this time. These include the clock tower and adjoining buildings, the almshouses, and

Fairford Area 143

"Keble's Bridge", Eastleach

several cottages, all designed to blend in with the older properties. Watercress from the beds by the Leach was once an Eastleach industry and was sent to the Midlands by train from Fairford Station.

Walkabout

1. From the road junction by the Victoria Inn, and with the clock tower on the right, walk down the village street. Keep right at the fork by the almshouses, down to the war memorial. This is a good vantage point to see the Leach, spanned by Keble's Bridge, with Eastleach Martin church beyond. Below to the right is the Victorian water fountain, while further downstream can be seen the 17th century Troutbeck Farmhouse, with its fine barns.

2. Cross Keble's Bridge and walk along the river bank to enter the churchyard. From here, Eastleach Turville can be seen climbing the opposite bank, with early 18th century Greenbury House dominating the scene, its later Gothick castellations and bay window prominent. Notice the remnants of a 14th century cross and the stone-tiled barn between the churchyard and neighbouring Bouthrop house (Bouthrop was once an alternative name for Eastleach Martin). The church is now in the care of the Churches Conservation Trust. Although Norman, it was rebuilt in the 13th century, when the striking windows were added.

3. Leave the churchyard by the top gate and turn left to cross the road bridge. Beyond, turn right to reach St Andrew's Church, with its distinctive saddleback tower. Hollies abound in the churchyard, as do cherubs' heads on the weathered tombstones. The church is entered through a beautiful 12th century doorway, surmounted by a tympanum depicting Christ in Majesty. Inside is a spacious early English chancel, in which is displayed a copy of John Keble's 'A Christian Year' and evidence of a north aisle and a chantry chapel.

4. To continue, walk back to the road and in a short distance, at the far corner of a long house, turn right and climb a flight of steps to reach a lane roughly parallel to the main street.

5. Turn right, passing Greenbury House, viewed earlier, and follow the winding lane all the way to its junction with the main street, reached down a slope beyond a bend. Turn left back to the start.

Southrop

Getting there:	Southrop lies 2 miles west of the A361 and 2½ miles north of Lechlade.
Park:	In the centre of the village, near the Swan Inn. (O.S. Landranger Sheet 163. GR 200034).
Introducing the village	Pronounced Sutherup by the locals, this modest little village is the last place of any consequence on the River Leach before it reaches the Thames at St John's Bridge, near Lechlade. Small and modest it may be but there is plenty to see here for all that. It is endowed with much fine building – church, manor house, inn, school, farms, barns, dovecote, cottages – with hardly a jarring sight to mar its beauty. And the beguiling little Leach, hurrying down from the Eastleaches and under the roadside willows on the final stage of its journey, adds its own touch of grace to complete the picture.
Refreshments:	The Swan Inn.

A peep into the past

The history of Southrop is closely linked with Oxford University. The manor was bought in 1612 by Dorothy Wadham, who gave it to the college she had founded. It remained the property of Wadham College for over 300 years. Before then, Sir Thomas Conway held the manor and his effigy, together with that of his lady, adorns the chancel of the church.

It was in this church that John Keble, while curate here, discovered the beautifully decorated Norman font walled up near the south doorway. This treasure, with its symbolic carvings depicting the Virtues trampling on the Vices, attracts visitors from far and wide.

Keble, author of 'The Christian Year', spent much of his working life at Hursley in Hampshire but it was at Southrop that, together with his friends Froude, Williams and Wilberforce, he founded the Oxford Movement. Keble College at Oxford is named after him.

Kebles had lived at Grey's Court in the 17th century and a monument to Thomas, who died in 1670, can be seen in the church.

Walkabout

Southrop is strung out along four wriggling country roads and the only way to explore it satisfactorily involves retracing steps. However, this entails no hardship for there is so much to see.

1. Follow the Filkins signpost. Dominating the vicarage garden on the right is a superb cedar of Lebanon, a silent witness to the founding of the Oxford Movement by John Keble and his friends during his curacy here (1823-5).

   Also on the right is another notable tree, this time a yew, shading the upper section of raised pavement opposite the school. Notice too the polypody fern thriving on the adjoining wall.

2. Still on the right, St Peter's Church is reached along a path leading also to Manor Farm. The little church, lacking a tower, is easily overlooked but ranks as one of the oldest and best preserved in Gloucestershire. As if that were not enough, it contains the Keble family monument, the Conway effigies and of course the exceptionally fine font.

Southrop church and farm approach

There is much to see from the church approach. On the left towers the 16th century manor house, said to have been connected to the church by an underground passage emerging from a false tomb in the chancel. On the gable of two of the outbuildings can be seen tiny turrets that may have been medieval lanterns.

Another immense building dwarfs the church on the right. This is one of Southrop's many fine barns. As the arrow on the nearby wall indicates, a public footpath crosses the farmyard, enabling this and adjacent buildings to be seen close up.

Before leaving the church, notice the patched old stable door of the porch, the Saxon-style herringbone stonework of the outer wall of the nave and the weathered group of tombs, including one of bale-top design, in the churchyard.

3. On the left, a short distance down the street, is the former corn mill, beautifully restored in the 1960s and now a private house.

4. Back at the start, walk along the Fairford road. In a short distance, on the left, is an 18th century house with a Georgian facade. Nearby is a barn incorporating a dovecote and topped by a lantern. Just beyond the village hall is a house with a traditional Cotswold bread oven.

5. Two interesting houses stand on the right of the Eastleach road. First is a remnant of a once larger house known as Grey's Court, home of the Kebles. A four gabled dovecote stands close by. The second house, Fyfield House, is early 18th century and like other houses of distinction in the village, has elegant ball finials to enhance its appeal.

Stroud and Tetbury Area

The south west Cotswolds differ markedly in character from the rest of the region. West of a line from the escarpment village of Birdlip southwards through Cirencester Park to the source of the Thames between Coates and Kemble, the landscape is one of high, bare uplands. These are intersected by steep narrow valleys, of which that of the River Frome, together with its tributaries, flowing westwards towards the Severn, is the most significant.

This valley, better known as the Stroud or Golden Valley, was the centre of the weaving industry that brought great prosperity to the region in bygone times. A cottage industry at first, it expanded later through the building of water-powered mills which employed thousands of hands in the production of high quality cloth such as Stroud scarlet and Uley blue.

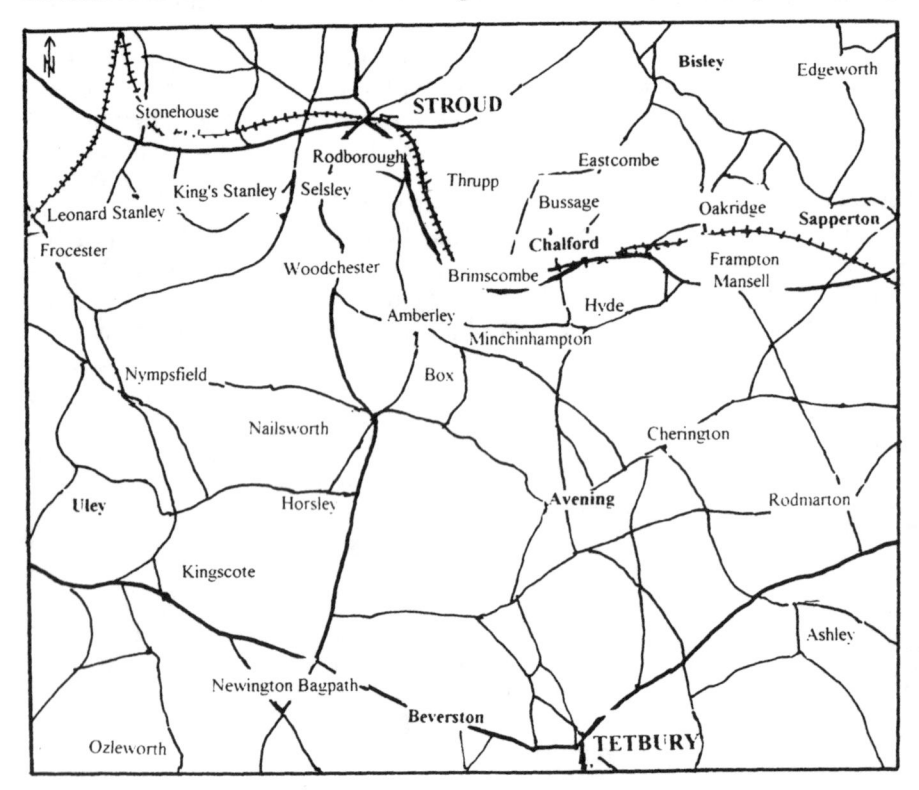

Although the surviving mills are now converted to other uses, and the Stroudwater and Thames canals dug in the late 18th century have long been abandoned, the villages of the Stroud and Nailsworth valleys retain their workaday appearance. Even so, such places as Uley and Chalford possess a charm of their own, while the upland villages, such as Bisley, Sapperton, Horsley and Nympsfield combine attractiveness with historical interest.

The uplands themselves, especially the National trust-owned commons of Rodborough and Minchinhampton, provide bracing walking and sweeping views, while for those wishing to tackle longer walks, a section of the Cotswold Way ascends Frocester Hill on its way northwards towards Painswick Beacon, with panoramic views westwards to the Severn and beyond.

Stroud and Tetbury

Stroud, a bustling industrial town of steeply climbing streets, sprawls at the junction of five narrow valleys, along which water-powered cloth mills formerly established it as the cloth weaving capital of the Cotswolds.

These mills, serving today in a range of capacities, are well worth studying, as is their history as revealed in the towns' excellent museum.

The area around Stroud is often referred to as 'Laurie Lee Country', on account of the close proximity of Slad, near Painswick, where the author was born and bred and which he described so eloquently in his autobiographical 'Cider with Rosie'.

A small elegant market town at the southern extremity of the area, Tetbury's prosperity came from the wool trade and its handsome church, 17th century market house and wide streets lined with good stone houses and inns reflect its past glory.

Avening

Getting there:	Avening stands on the B4014, 2 miles S.E. of Nailsworth.
Park:	Off the B4014, as near as possible to the church. (O.S. Landranger Sheet 162. GR 880981)
Introducing the village	Avening is the only village astride the B4014 on its tortuous six-mile journey from Nailsworth to Tetbury. This road, built by the Nailsworth Valley Turnpike Trust in the 1780s, climbs from Nailsworth along the wooded valley of the Avening Stream, which supplied the power to drive the mills that brought prosperity to the village. Some of the mill buildings survive, as do the fine houses built by the millowners and these, together with much else of interest, can be seen on the village walkabout.
Refreshments:	Bell Inn. Cross Inn.

A peep into the past

Standing stones, tumps and long barrows litter the high wolds around Avening, a reminder that the village has rich archaeological associations. However, the earliest known inhabitant was Britric, a Saxon nobleman who, while on a visit to Flanders, met Matilda, the ruler's daughter, whose advances he rejected. Years later, as queen to William the Conqueror, Matilda was able to wreak her revenge by having Britric imprisoned and his estate confiscated. On hearing of her victim's death in prison, the Queen, in remorse, is said to have ordered the building of the present church, possibly replacing a Saxon one on the same site.

A quaint custom, Pig Face Sunday, was formerly celebrated at Avening. Supposedly it originated from the feast given by Matilda to the builders following the consecration of the church and was celebrated on the nearest Sunday to 14th September. Brawn made from pigs' heads was eaten and a dramatic re-enactment of the visit of Queen Matilda took place.

Avening Mill, dating from 1706, was built for fulling cloth by William Gyde. It was the highest of several mills erected on the Avening Stream. The present building consists of 4 storeys and is of early 19th century origin, having been built by William Playne, a member of a prominent local mill-owning family. It has served as a corn mill and for the manufacture of silk. It is now a centre for light industry and offices.

Stroud and Tetbury Area 151

Avening from the top road

Walkabout

This is somewhat longer than usual – about 1.75 miles – and is partly along quiet lanes with wide views.

1. The Church of the Holy Cross stands well in its sloping churchyard. It dates from 1080 and its consecration is said to have taken place in the presence of Queen Matilda, wife of William the Conqueror, for reasons explained earlier. Fortunately, every effort was made during the restoration of 1902 to preserve the distinctive Norman features, which include superb stone vaulting, chancel arch and north doorway. In the north transept can be seen a monument to Henry Bridges of Avening Court, son of Lord Chandos of Sudeley Castle, Winchcombe, who after a notorious career as a pirate and highwayman, was pardoned by James 1, returned to his native Gloucestershire and married the daughter of Samuel Sheppard, a wealthy Avening clothier. Dated 1615, the monument depicts the reformed outlaw in effigy, kneeling at prayer, humble and penitent.

The church is rich in memorials and assorted relics of Avening's ancient and more recent past.

2. From the church, pass the school and memorial hall and turn right by the Bell Inn up New Inn Lane. This climbs steeply past some handsome old houses before swinging to the left to rejoin the High Street, though not before providing sweeping views across the valley.

3. Continue to reach the Cross, now merely a meeting of ways, presided over by an appropriately named inn and with an appealing pinnacled fountain erected in 1896 in memory of a much-respected villager, William Fowles.

4. Leave the main road here, proceeding down the hill to the left of the inn. At the foot of the slope, opposite the Old Hill sign, turn right up Mays Lane. Before rejoining the Minchinhampton road, this lane provides glimpses of 16th century Avening Court and of the beautiful gardens laid out along the Avening Stream.

5. Back at the main road, cross straight over and follow the public footpath down to Old Lane. Turn right. Pass the clear-running spring on the right, reached by steps. Turn left along Rectory Lane. Beyond houses, good views can be had to the left of Avening Mill and of the church. Follow Rectory Lane to its end, at the foot of a slope leading to the B4014. Cross back to the start.

Beverston

Getting there:	Beverston lies off the A4135, 1½ miles west of Tetbury.
Park:	By the church. (O.S. Landranger Sheet 163. GR 096340)
Introducing the village	Cotswold villages seldom come tinier than this but for those to whom small means beautiful, Beverston is a gem. The sense of relief with which the visitor pulls off the main road into what passes for Beverston's one and only street, is as nothing compared with the discovery of this trim little village. For not only is it well kept and attractive in the best Cotswold tradition but it boasts a link with the past that none of its fellow villages can match – the romantic ruin of a castle. A little of Beverston spills out along the relentless A4135, and a not-to-be-missed green, fringed by more good looking buildings, is severed from the village by the same racetrack of a road. There is no pub, no shop, no school. But there is plenty to compensate for those who find pleasure in lingering in out-of-the-way places.
Refreshments:	A choice of pubs and teashops in Tetbury.

A peep into the past

A castle of some sort existed at Beverston in Saxon times. In 1051, Earl Godwin and Harold (later of Hastings fame) stayed here and the carving of Christ on the church tower suggests that an earlier church stood here too.

The present castle dates from about 1225 and originally had four drum towers arranged round a quadrangle. By the 15th century it had been enlarged and given a gatehouse and a drawbridge to provide access over a moat. It was held for the king during the Civil War but its commander, Colonel Oglethorpe, was so preoccupied with his courtship of a local beauty that he neglected his duties and his army fled, leaving the advancing Parliamentarian forces to capture the castle.

Considerable rebuilding was carried out after a damaging fire in 1691, but although the inhabited part of the building has been well maintained and a recent addition made, the castle proper is a ruin and is not normally open to visitors.

By the early 1800s, the church, too, had fallen into a state of disrepair and it was not until the 1840s, when R.S. Holford of Westonbirt bought the estate, that restoration work began. This was carried out by Lewis Vulliamy, designer of Westonbirt House and Dorchester House in Park

Lane, London, who later went on to design many of the houses fronting the Tetbury-Dursley road.

Beverston Castle

Walkabout

1. As this begins near St Mary's Church, visitors may wish to start their tour here. In fact, its oldest feature can be glimpsed from the road – a late Saxon stone carving of Christ, set high on the south face of the tower. Inside the church are more ancient stone carvings, this time 13th century coffin lids with incised crosses, built into the north wall. Dominating the nave is a beautiful 13th century 3-bay arcade, while the chancel contains a fine rood screen that was rescued from the rectory garden after being used as a pergola.

2. The castle can be viewed from several different angles. Beyond the church the remains of the moat are clearly visible, while the best overall view is through the main entrance. The upper walls afford perfect nesting sites for jackdaws, the raucous calls of which reach their peak after the young are fledged in late spring.

3. Continue towards the main road, passing the veteran walnut tree, propped up by old power poles. Beyond, on the left, is an ancient low stone barn, believed to be 700 years old, supported by buttresses and comprising five bays. The story goes that it provided shelter to medieval pilgrims on their way to Malmesbury Abbey.

4. Cross the A4135 and follow the lane round the green, in the centre of which stands a veteran yew tree. The handsome buildings of Park Farm can be seen on the right.

5. Cross the main road once more by the memorial garden. Notice the mid 19th century estate cottages designed for Robert Holford by Lewis Vulliamy, with their Gothic porches and characteristic finials.

6. Follow the narrow lane directly opposite. Beyond the cottages, this becomes a grassy path leading back almost to the start.

Bisley

Getting there:	Bisley lies 2 miles north of the A419, 4 miles east of Stroud.
Park:	On George Street, climbing from High Street. Below the Bear Inn and opposite the lock-up. (O.S. Landranger Sheet 163. GR 903060).
Introducing the village	A large village in a scattered parish, high above the Frome Valley, Bisley is a tangle of narrow streets and twisting lanes, ideal for leisurely on-foot exploration. Good Cotswold stone buildings abound. They range from All Saints' Church, its lofty spire dominating the surrounding landscape, to splendid houses representing many periods, together with a host of equally charming cottages ranging up and down the steeply climbing ways. Add to all this the delightful views that open out at the summit of every rise and Bisley emerges as one of the most alluring destinations in a region renowned for the outstanding quality of its villages.
Refreshments:	Bear Inn. Stirrup Cup Inn.

A peep into the past

The hills around Bisley are strewn with barrows and other evidence of prehistoric settlement. Later, the Romans built a large villa near the present village. The Bisley we see today is largely the product of the boom years of the Cotswold cloth trade, during which wealthy clothiers built themselves fine houses using the abundant local limestone.

Lean years followed, with 'Beggarly Bisley' featuring in a local rhyme. By Victorian times, however, things were looking up and the Thomas Kebles, father and son rectors, between them restored the church and established the Ascension Day well-dressing tradition.

It is to Thomas Keble junior that we owe the legend of the Bisley Boy. After the discovery of the skeleton of a young girl during the excavation of the foundations of the school, he concocted a tale in which the young Princess Elizabeth died while staying in the village. To avoid the wrath of Henry VIII, her place was taken by a local boy, who eventually became 'Queen' of England!

Walkabout

1. This starts with the Bear Inn. This distinctive building, with its elegant stone columns supporting the upper floor, was formerly a

Stroud and Tetbury Area 157

court house. Notice the ornate curved lintel over the side door and the mounting block alongside.

2. The twin-cell lock-up, like everything else in Bisley, was done with style. Dated 1824, it is nicely gabled and topped with a ball finial. Even so, one suspects that these refinements were wasted on the unfortunate inmates. Close by, let into the wall, is a rare milestone, proclaiming 'Gloster X miles'.

3. Walk down George Street towards High Street. A short distance before the junction, turn right along a lane by Parson's Cottage, to reach the churchyard. To the right of the main church door is a weathered monument, dating from the 13th century. It is a well head known as a poor soul's light, so called because candles for the poor

Poor Soul's Light

were once lit in the openings during mass. Said to be the only one of its kind, it is known locally as the bonehouse, on account of the story that before its construction, a priest fell to his death down the uncovered well one dark night.

The 18th century gazebo in the churchyard wall nearby belongs to Over Court, a magnificent medieval house visible through a handgate in the wall. It was in this garden that the stone coffin containing the bones of the young girl was found in the 1850s, and which gave rise to the story of the Bisley Boy.

4. A visit to the church will be greatly enhanced by the purchase of a copy of the guide, excellent value at 50p. Though heavily restored in the 1860s, the church contains much of interest, in particular the richly decorated Norman foot with two fish carved inside the bowl. There is also a striking effigy of a 13th century knight in chain mail and a brass to Kateryn Sewell, who died in 1515.

5. Follow the churchyard wall down to the steps, which lead to a lane. Turn right and keep to the right for a short distance for a glimpse of 18th century Jaynes Court, with its unusual octagonal building, combining a dovecote with a cockpit.

6. Retrace back to the foot of the steps and continue along the lane. The wells, with their gabled water chutes, are on the left. Keep left at a fork, to reach the High Street.

7. Turn left up the street, noticing the former Bell Inn, now the British Legion, on the left. Wesley House, of 16th century origin, is on the same side. Continue to regain George Street, which branches to the left opposite the post office.

Chalford

Getting there:	Chalford lies off the A419, 3 miles SE of Stroud.
Park:	In lay-by alongside the A419 between the church and the junction with High Street. (O.S. Landranger Sheet 163. GR 893025).
Introducing the village	Chalford, a tangle of zigzagging lanes and paths rising abruptly from the floor of the Golden Valley, is a difficult place to explore. Workaday, yet set in superb scenery, it is a relic of the boom years of the Cotswold cloth industry, with mills lining the valley, weavers' cottages clinging to terraces at every conceivable level, and the former homes of wealthy clothiers dotted around in spacious gardens and commanding impressive views. Lacking an obvious centre, Chalford is above all else, a walker's village. Its steep, narrow roads are totally unsuitable for cars. So leave yours in the lay-by, brace yourself for some challenging gradients, and savour to the full the nearest thing to a mountain village that the Cotswolds can offer.
Refreshments:	New Red Lion Inn, High Street.

A peep into the past

The valley of the River Frome is said to have been called the Golden Valley, not on account of its beauty, but because of the wealth generated along its course during the time when the Cotswolds led the world in cloth manufacture. The weavers have gone but the name Rack Hill survives, indicating the area where they once spread their drying racks and tenters.

Although the construction of the Thames-Severn Canal in the 1780s brought new trading opportunities, bales of woven cloth were still for a time transported by donkey power up the narrow winding paths from the weavers' cottages to distant locations.

Later, huge mills were built along the valley floor, several of which, converted to other uses, can still be seen today. In time the donkeys' work was restricted to carrying panniers of coal and groceries up the paths to isolated cottages.

Although Chalford had its own Anglican church by 1724, the number of chapels of different denominations indicates that nonconformity was strong among the weaving community. In 1739, over 3,000 people gathered to hear George Whitfield, a prominent Gloucester preacher.

Like the mills it once served, the Thames-Severn Canal went into

Chalford canal and "roundhouse"

decline in the late 19th century. Water loss had always been a problem and with the closure of the port of Brimscombe and the partial collapse of the Sapperton tunnel, its days as a trading waterway were over.

Today, the towpath enables walkers to explore what was once one of the most prosperous parts of the Cotswolds.

Walkabout

1. From the lay-by, walk along the pavement for the short distance to reach High Street. Beyond the post office, climb the path with a handrail just before Corner House. (The New Red Lion Inn, visible ahead, will be passed later on the canal towpath).

2. Keep on along the upper path. Pass a chapel below, and at a junction, take the higher path to reach a flight of steps by a cottage ('Hillside').

3. Turn right, pass Manse Cottage, and follow the now almost level path to reach a road, with the Baptist Tabernacle on the left. Turn right. An excellent view of the High Street opens out away to the right. At the foot of the slope, turn left by the post-box. A fine 17th century house, The Mount, stands to the left here, with Green Court opposite.

4. On reaching a fork, bear right towards the bridge over the canal. The distinctive house by the bridge was once the Valley Inn.

5. Follow the towpath to the right. The canal is now on the left and the little River Frome on the right.

6. On reaching the A419, cross with care to regain the towpath. On the left now are the former Bliss Mills. Emerging at the A419 once more, turn left along the verge and in 30 metres, go left again along the Hyde and Minchinhampton road. A former canal lengthman's round house soon appears on the right, while opposite is a fascinating old building, said to have been a manor house when built in the 15th century. Later it became the Company's Arms Inn, in which the East India Company buyers traded.

7. Climb to the canal towpath, from which good views can be had of Belvedere Mill and its pond, together with two ancient iron boilers. By the towpath, and mounted on a stone base, are cogwheels from the sluice of the former Seville's Mill. There is also a useful information board outlining the history of the canal.

8. Follow the towpath to the right, passing the round house, back to the A419. Cross to regain the lay-by.

Sapperton

Getting there:	Sapperton lies 1 mile north of the A419, 8 miles east of Stroud.
Park:	Along the lane leading past the church. (O.S. Landranger sheet 163. GR 948035).
Introducing the village	Few Cotswold villages as modest in size as Sapperton offer as much to interest the visitor as this village, perched high above the beautiful wooded Frome Valley between Stroud and Cirencester. For Sapperton boasts not only a distinctive church and a good share of other buildings skilfully fashioned from the local limestone, but its history is linked with that of one of Gloucestershire's finest parks, with a late 18th century canal connecting the Thames with the Severn, and with the revival of traditional crafts. The village is also associated with two remarkable books. It was a Sapperton man, Sir Robert Atkyns, who, early in the 18th century, wrote the first history of Gloucestershire, while in 1986, the headmistress and children of Sapperton school published 'Village Heritage', their own award-winning account of the history of their village.
Refreshments:	Bell Inn, Sapperton. Daneway Inn (half a mile west).

A peep into the past

Sapperton's past is inextricably bound up with that of Cirencester Park. In 1730, the first Lord Bathurst bought and demolished Sapperton Hall, the manor house of the Pooles, and later of the Atkyns, and extended his great park as far as the village. Stone from the house was used to create the mock ruin, Alfred's Hall, within the park.

In 1789, a two-mile-long tunnel was driven from Daneway, west of the village, to carry the new Thames-Severn canal beneath Sapperton to Coates. The navvies' inn, now known as the Daneway, still stands by the abandoned waterway and the tunnel's north portal can be reached by footpath from near the churchyard gate.

It was at Daneway House nearby that early in the 20th century, Ernest Gimson and the Barnsley brothers established their first workshop. Inspired by the Arts and Crafts movement pioneered by William Morris, they were largely responsible for ensuring that the Cotswolds commanded a prominent place in the revival of quality craftsmanship using a wide range of local materials.

Sapperton church

Walkabout

1. St Kenelm's Church makes the obvious starting place. Before entering the building however, there are the graves of Sapperton's three famous craftsmen to see beneath the churchyard yews. To the left of the sloping path is the grave of Ernest Gimson, who died in 1919, while opposite lie his friends Ernest and Sidney Barnsley. The incised brass plates on their graves continue a tradition dating from the 17th century. As well as several well preserved ornately decorated headstones, the churchyard also contains the remains of an early 15th century cross.

The interior of the church is a fascinating mixture of many periods. Originally Norman, St Kenelm's was rebuilt in the 14th century, modified during Tudor times, and finally rebuilt around 1705, after which it was refurnished with intricately carved panelling taken from the demolished hall. Of the monuments, two in particular are worth seeing. These are those of Sir Henry Poole (died 1616) and his family, with kneeling effigies in marble, and Sir Robert Atkyns, author of 'The Ancient and Present State of Gloucestershire', who died in 1711 and who is depicted reclining, appropriately with a book.

2. Back at the churchyard gate, turn right and walk along the street. Away to the right, above the rooftops of the cottages clinging to the lower slopes, the beechwoods across the Frome Valley make a perfect backdrop. Continue past the school to a crossroads.

3. Turn left to reach the spacious green. The cottages on the left were built by Ernest Barnsley, while Batchelor's Court, the steeply gabled house straight ahead, with its fine yew topiary work, was the home of Norman Jewson, who worked with Gimson and the Barnsleys and wrote about his life at Sapperton in his book 'By Chance I did Rove'.

Away to the right can be seen one of several beech-clad mounds formed by spoil from the shafts of the canal tunnel which passes beneath the village.

4. Turn left by Batchelor's Court back to the street. Turn right and retrace to the junction by the church. To see the Bell Inn and other interesting buildings, turn right again. The village hall, on the right, was built by Ernest Barnsley in 1912. A fine 17th century house stands higher up the slope, also on the right.

Stroud and Tetbury Area

Uley and Owlpen

Getting there:	Uley lies on the B4066, 7 miles SW of Stroud.
Park:	In the vicinity of the green and the Old Crown Inn. (O.S. Landranger Sheet 162. GR 793987).
Introducing the villages	Uley is essentially a single-street village, strung out along the winding B4066 as it descends to the Ewelme Valley and Dursley from the high wolds south of Stroud. Handsome clothiers' houses line this road and there are more tucked away from view along inviting little side lanes, while to the north of the village are two of the most notable prehistoric features in the entire Cotswolds. A mile distant is the lovely 15th century manor house of Owlpen, with its church close by. All this indicates plenty of historical interest hereabouts and an on-foot exploration of Uley and neighbourhood cannot fail to be rewarding.
Refreshments:	Old Crown Inn. King's Head Inn. Pumps Restaurant.

A peep into the past

Uley's earliest known inhabitants were the fifteen Neolithic folk whose skeletons were discovered during the 19th century within Hetty Pegler's Tump, a chambered barrow a mile or so to the north of the village.

It was Uley's Iron Age people who constructed the great hill fort above the village. Known as Uley Bury, this 32-acre earthwork is the finest of its kind in Gloucestershire and its outer rampart makes a spectacular circular walk.

Uley village itself developed, like its neighbours, as a cloth-weaving town. John Eyles began weaving Spanish cloth at Uley in the 17th century and soon clothiers were wealthy enough to build themselves the fine houses we see today. In time, a cottage industry gave way to factories and the boom in Uley Blue cloth lasted until the early 19th century. Hard times followed. The closure of Shepherd's Mill in 1837 threw 1000 people out of work. Many emigrated. Others trekked to the coal mines of South Wales.

Today, with its neighbour, Owlpen, Uley enjoys quiet prosperity in a corner of the south Cotswolds, surprisingly undiscovered by all but the discerning visitor.

Walkabout

The Street, Uley's main thoroughfare, is wide and offers good views of the well-wooded local landscape so that, despite the traffic and the need to retrace steps, the walkabout is pleasant throughout.

Uley

1. The Green, from which the walkabout begins, is flanked to the north by elegant houses, chiefly Georgian in period and set in ample gardens. Adjacent to the strangely named Fiery Lane, leading to Owlpen, is a row of attractive cottages and the Old Crown Inn.

2. St Giles's Church, a complete rebuilding, dates from 1857 and commands the village from its steep bank. Inside is an artist's impression (dated 1830) of the old church it replaced. Perhaps the most interesting feature is the flat tombstone in the churchyard overlooking the

road. It marks the grave of Roger Rutter, alias Rudder, the father of Samuel, the Gloucestershire historian, who was buried on 30th August 1771, aged 84 after "having never eaten Flesh, Fish nor Fowl during the course of his long life".

Uley's distinctive buildings are not confined to houses. Even the two 1949 bus shelters, one of which faces the church, have elegant stone pillars.

3. Walk down the right-hand pavement of the Street. Notice No. 49, just after the post office – a steeply gabled house possessing classic Cotswold features. Further down, by contrast, in a builder's yard, is a quaint tin barn with what must surely be the most irregular wooden posts imaginable!

4. Where the pavement ends, by Court House, turn right to see the early 18th century Weaver's House, with its sundial prominent on the corner. Next comes the Old Brewery, still operating and with 'Price 1833' indicating its origin.

5. Keep to the left along Whitecourt. Beyond the former chapel, dated 1790, keep left along the sunken Fop Street, passing the excellent 18th century Combe House on the right, to reach The Street once more. Ahead is Stout's Hill, built as a mansion for a wealthy clothier in 1743 and now a timeshare property.

6. Turn left along the high pavement. The King's Head is early 18th century. To see the unusual former Bethesda Chapel of 1821, and now an arts centre, cross by the novel Pumps Restaurant and walk down South Street. The old chapel yard, in which wood sculptures stand alongside tomb stones, is on the left.

7. Retrace to the start. Both Owlpen and Uley Bury can be reached by footpaths (see OS Landranger 162) or alternatively by road. Hetty Pegler's Tump is approached by footpath from the B4066.

Appendix

Recommended Reading

'Gloucestershire. The Cotswolds. Buildings of England Series' David Verey. Penguin.

'Buildings of the Cotswolds' Denis Moriarty. Gollancz.

'The Cotswolds' Josceline Finberg. Eyre Methuen.

'The Cotswolds' Anthea Jones. Phillimore.

'Cotswold Villages' June Lewis. Hale.

'The Gloucestershire Village Book' Countryside Books & G.F.W.I.

'Hidden Gloucestershire' Margaret Sollars. Countryside Books.

'The Cotswolds. A New Study.' C & A.M. Hadfield. David & Charles.

'Gloucestershire Countryside' Gordon Ottewell. Minton & Minton.

Tourist Information in the Cotswolds

Broadway: 1, Cotswold Court – (01386-852937)

Burford: The Brewery, Sheep Street – (01993-823558)

Cheltenham: 77, Promenade – (01242-522878)

Chipping Campden: Noel Arms Hotel, High Street – (01386-841206)

Cirencester: Corn Hall, Market Place – (01285-654180)

Northleach: Cotswold Countryside Collection – (01451-60715)

Painswick: The Library, Stroud Road – (01452-813552)

Stow-on-the-Wold: Hollis House, The Square – (01451-31082)

Stroud: The Subscription Rooms, George Street – (01453-765768)

Tetbury: The Old Court House, 63, Long Street – (01666-503552)

Winchcombe: Town Hall, High Street – (01242-602925)